A Family No More

Amy Quonce

ISBN-13: 978-0-9890904-2-1
ISBN-10: 0989090426

Library of Congress Control Number: 2016904645

Cover design by TWA Solutions
www.twasoltuions.com

ACKNOWLEDGMENTS

A very sincere thank you to my friends and fellow authors at the Carolina Forest writers group. Your expertise, wisdom, and guidance allowed this book to flourish.

CHAPTER ONE

May 2000

He couldn't have been more than eleven. His round prepubescent face still contained a hint of childlike youth, yet the erratic behaviors the boy displayed detracted from his innocent features. With arms stretched outright, strategically placed at ten and two, he maneuvered an imaginary steering wheel in the direction of anyone he could find and shouted obscenities at them. His mother, obviously embarrassed, tried to quiet him from her chair, but his only response was to turn the wheel in her direction and pretend to run her over.

Kate discretely shook her head, ignored the duo the best she could, and continued to leaf through an outdated copy of *People* magazine. *How did we get to this point?*

"Mrs. Rose, the doctor can see you now," the tall receptionist with wavy black hair cascading half-way down her back called.

Kate put the magazine back on the shelf, picked up her purse, and walked toward Dr. Covington's office as his ten o'clock appointment abruptly brushed past her on his way out. Tall, well groomed, and wearing an Armani Polo shirt and tan khakis, the child certainly presented himself well. At first glance, it would be hard for an outsider to discern there were issues of any kind. But as his mother, Kate knew looks could be deceiving.

Andrew didn't even glance in her direction as they passed, but proceeded toward the waiting room in a casual strut. Kate turned her head to remind him to behave himself until she came back out, but he had already plopped himself down across from road-rage boy and took pleasure in helping him navigate toward unsuspecting pedestrians. Sighing, she followed the psychologist through the door. They walked silently into his office, as if conversation at that point would be taboo.

Kate sat gingerly on the sleek black leather couch, biting her nails until the tender skin came exposed. Dr. Covington quietly looked over his notes before making eye contact.

"Mrs. Rose," he began after review of the files, "I have been seeing Andrew three times a week for the past twelve weeks. In our time together, I have gotten to know him quite well. I can tell you one thing for sure; your son is very intelligent. Andrew can be charming, engaging, and is quite skilled in his verbal language." He inhaled, as if what was coming next wasn't as easy to say. "But, I can also tell you there is a lot more hiding behind his fake smile. Your son is devious, manipulative, and has a preoccupation with violence. He displays no empathy toward others and avoids personal connections at all costs."

The straight-forwardness of his remarks startled Kate. *That's why we're here. You're the leading child psychologist in the state. Please help our family.*

Dr. Covington flipped back through his thick piles of notes he had accumulated through the past three months.

"During our time together, I have gained Andrew's trust and he has confided some very disturbing things to me. Due to doctor/patient privilege I cannot disclose what he has said, but I can tell you I am extremely concerned for your daughter, Megan."

The blood instantly drained from Kate's face. Megan, who was two years younger than Andrew, had been diagnosed with high functioning autism at the age of three. This had sent them on an intense path of constant doctor appointments, as well as a spectrum of therapists who worked diligently with her in attempt to get Megan on level with other kids her age. With so much focus spent on her daughter's needs, she knew Andrew had been vying for attention in mischievous ways. "What about her?" she whispered in fear.

Dr. Covington straightened himself in the chair as his face grew serious. "As I said before, all I can do is voice my concerns. You've told me Megan's autism left her speechless for the first six years of life. This trademark silence gave Andrew plenty of opportunities to do as he pleased without concern of her telling on him."

Kate's hands shook as she buried her head within them. She was torn between wanting to know what went on during those silent years, and pretending Andrew would never hurt his little sister. It took her a few moments before she could look up and meet the doctor's eyes. "What are you saying?" she asked, not really wanting to hear the answer.

Placing a gentle hand on hers, Dr. Covington continued. "Mrs. Rose, Andrew is cruel and aggressive. His behaviors are combined with a self-righteous approach to getting his needs met. He has significant psychiatric concerns, and his willingness to harm others has left him void of empathy, compassion, and without significant attachments."

"What can I do to help him?" Kate pleaded.

Dr. Covington sighed and shook his head. "We're doing all we can, but his progress in therapy has been minimal. I'm sorry to say this Mrs. Rose, but your child shows all the classical signs of being a sociopath. One day he's going to do something that will land him at the mercy of the court system. My best guess is that he won't get the level of help he truly needs until then."

Her heart ached to refute those words. The realization that she might face something far worse than behavior problems terrified her. "It's hard enough worrying about Megan every day," Kate admitted, "but I also fear for the children at school."

The doctor leaned in closer and adjusted his glasses for a better view. "Why are you afraid for them?" he asked.

Kate swallowed, embarrassed at what she had to tell him. "I got a phone call from Andrew's school the other day. Apparently, he sprayed a child with cologne, and then attempted to light a lighter in hopes of catching him on fire."

It was hard for Kate not to notice Dr. Covington's eyes widening in disbelief. "Did anybody get hurt?"

Shaking her head, she answered quickly while trying to fight back the tears that were starting to well up in her throat. "Thankfully it didn't ignite, but the school told me it terrified the poor kid. Andrew received a two-day suspension for his actions."

Dr. Covington passed Kate a tissue box and waited silently as she wept away the frustration that had been building up since Andrew had been a tiny boy. Once she composed herself, he set his notebook down and moved closer to her chair. "Why do you keep putting up with this?" he asked.

Kate didn't hesitate with her answer. "It's my job as a parent and I love him," she cried.

"It's also your job as a parent to protect your daughter," he added, looking her straight in the eyes. "You've told me over the years Andrew has been smearing feces on the walls and has injured the cat on more than one occasion, in addition to hurting other children. Plus, you've stated your family cringes when you bring him to their homes because they never know what is going to happen." He took a long pause to allow Kate enough time to absorb his words before continuing. "Why are you willing to risk everything in your life that you love, for only one thing you love?"

Reaching for another tissue, Kate tried to find a reasonable answer in her head. What she came up with, however, was brutal truth. "What are my choices? I can't throw him out on the street," she asserted.

Folding his arms across his chest, Dr. Covington gave Kate a no-nonsense look. "He has a father. Since he claims he has no problems with Andrew, let him take him."

"I don't know," she replied shaking her head. "Ed has a terrible temper. Plus, he barely wants to take the kids for visitations, let alone raise one full-time."

"Promise me you'll think about it, at least for Megan's sake," he urged.

Kate leaned forward and offered a nod. Dr. Covington patted her shoulder, and then stood to guide her to the receptionist desk so she could make Andrew's next appointment. When she finished, she walked silently out to gather up her son and her coat. Still in shock, she only gestured to Andrew to follow her back out to the car.

The ten-minute drive back to Belleview Elementary School felt unusually long. Kate signed Andrew in, handed the secretary his doctor's excuse for being late, then rushed back to her car. Dr. Covington's words and a thousand other memories entered her mind to fill the silence. She couldn't help but to recall the countless times when Andrew had physically assaulted Megan, merely because she existed. A multitude of painful memories kept crashing in like angry waves during a storm.

Kate remembered the time when Megan was four-years-old and had mysteriously fallen into the pool. Andrew proudly boasted how he had jumped in to save her from drowning. He claimed he didn't want anything to happen to his little sister, so he saved her life. Kate told him he deserved a hero's party for his gallant gesture.

She also couldn't forget the steaming hot summer morning when Megan disappeared, and Andrew helped frantically search the house for her. Only upon hearing his mother mention she planned to call the cops for help did Andrew have the idea to look outside, and they found Megan passed out in the back seat of the car, sweating profusely and naked. In the moment, Kate praised Andrew for saving his sister once again, yet she couldn't shake the feeling of knowing something wasn't quite right; Megan had not yet mastered opening car doors, and would not have been able to get in there by herself.

Had Andrew been intentionally putting his sister in harm's way, and then making it look like he was protecting her for the praise? What else has Andrew confessed to that made Dr. Covington so worried for her safety?

Once Megan learned to talk, she often came crying to her mother saying Andrew had hurt her in some way or another. It seemed it always happened the moment Kate turned her back. Andrew always managed to calculate the perfect moment when no one was looking to perpetrate the acts, ergo no witnesses. When confronted, he'd stare his mother straight in the eye, intensely proclaiming his innocence. For his young age, he grew to be a very skilled liar. As his mother, Kate knew she couldn't sit idle allowing this to continue.

Is choosing to allow my son to stay with me worth my daughter's safety? Would his behaviors grow worse under the influence of his father?

Ed Preston had a reputation for being a pompous, rage-fueled, arrogant man, and Kate blamed her ex-husband for many of Andrew's behaviors. While hesitant at the thought of him raising Andrew, she had to weigh her options carefully. For several weeks, she mulled over the ramifications of splitting up the kids.

The decision to let Andrew live with his father was not one Kate entered into easily. It only came after she convinced herself if he lived with Ed, she would be protecting more than her daughter. It would be allowing Andrew the opportunity to distance himself from the constant attention his special needs sister required, and his father would be able to give him more individual attention. With a heavy heart, Kate asked her ex-husband if he would be willing to let his son live with him.

As she packed up Andrew's belongings for the move, visions of him as a little boy flowed through her mind. They played over and over like a movie reel in her head. The day she brought him home snuggled tightly in his tiny, blue receiving blanket. When he took his first steps at nine-months-old. The angelic look on his face the day he came to visit Megan in the hospital after she was born. Now, twelve years later, she had to move him out of the house in a desperate attempt to do the right thing for both her children.

Kate could only hope her maternal instincts were guiding her in the right direction.

CHAPTER TWO

February 2001

The snow blew so fiercely Kate could barely make out the road markers on the side of the pavement. It was a white-knuckle drive, though not uncommon for wintertime in upstate New York. She turned the wipers up higher and strained her eyes to see through the large heavy snowflakes. A snowstorm wasn't going to interrupt a weekend visit with her son.

She made the trip every Friday night since Andrew moved in with his father the previous May, but tonight she wasn't in the mood to fight the weather. All Kate wanted to do was get back and relax in the safety of her home. She had momentarily considered calling to say she would pick him up the next weekend instead, but had already promised him she was coming, and didn't want to rescind her word. Their relationship had been rocky ever since the transition; Andrew believed she had chosen his sister over him. As a mom, Kate needed to prove to her son he was still an important part of her life, no matter where he lived.

When Kate and Megan arrived at Ed's house, they found Andrew home alone, as he always seemed to be; slumped on the couch, flipping through television channels without even glancing up as they walked in.

As a mother, she always loved the thought of bringing her son home and nurturing him to no end so he could remember what it was like to have someone care for him. For months, Ed and Kate argued back and forth over how much Andrew was left alone. Kate felt since he was only twelve-years-old, he was much too young and immature to be left on his own for long periods of time. Ed, however, saw no harm in it and continued to leave Andrew alone on a regular basis, sometimes even as long as a whole weekend. Kate made a mental note to once again speak with her ex-husband on the subject, and then set her purse down on the counter to help Andrew load his things into the car.

"Are all your bags packed?" Kate asked. "It's storming out and I want to get home as soon as possible."

Andrew Preston, who was growing up to be a carbon-copy of his father, shot her a dirty look. "No, my bags aren't packed," he snorted.

"Why not?" Kate snapped, without meaning to. She hated taking a tone with him, but couldn't help recognize the all-too-familiar war between them brewing.

"Because I'm not going with you, that's why," he shouted, slumping further down onto the couch.

Kate tried to calm herself before things got out of hand. "What do you mean you're not going with me?" she pressed, trying to soothe her voice as she spoke.

Andrew wasn't falling for her 'talk calmly to the kid and get a calm response' tactic. He wanted to take it to the next level. "You heard me. I AM NOT GOING. Is that clear enough for you, Mother?" he screamed.

That was all it took for Kate to completely lose her cool. "What is your problem?" she yelled back at him through clenched jaws.

Andrew's eyes grew big and icy. He stared his mother straight in the face and gave her an explanation he knew she wouldn't want to hear. "You are my problem. I already told you I'm not going and you won't leave me alone."

Kate hauled in a deep breath then let it out slowly as she mentally counted to three. "Your sister and I drove forty minutes in the middle of a storm to get you. You knew I was coming. Why didn't you call ahead and tell me you wanted to stay here if you didn't want to come?"

Andrew stretched back on the couch, resting both hands behind his head and deviously smiled. "Because, I wanted to see you waste your time," he grinned.

Six years of early childhood courses trained Kate well enough to know he was testing her. She quickly shifted her own attitude in hopes of redirecting his. "Go get yourself ready," she calmly ordered and tossed his over-night bag on the couch next to him so he could pack it. He stared intensely at her, refusing to budge an inch.

Without a word, Kate picked his bag back up and filled it with clothes from the laundry basket sitting near the coffee table. Andrew remained on the couch, still as a statue. The only flinch he made was to divert his eyes as Megan passed by on her way to look at her favorite Blue Gourami fish that always swam in circles around the fifty-five-gallon tank. Kate smiled at her daughter as she watched in awe of the sea creatures, and then headed down the hall to Andrew's room to find his snow boots.

As soon as Kate turned the handle to his bedroom door, she could hear the crying echoing behind her. Immediately, she rushed back down the hall to see what was wrong. Megan ran into her arms, holding her hand on her left cheek. "Andrew hit me in the face!" she sobbed. A bright red silhouette of her brother's hand glowed against her fair skin.

"I did not," he shouted back. "She's lying!"

Kate glared at him. He stared back; the rage in his eyes escalating.

"I am not spending the weekend this way!" Kate screamed, losing all resolve to remain calm. "Now apologize to her," she demanded.

Andrew crossed his arms, and raised an eyebrow at her. He wanted to assert his dominance, and see how far he could push his mother. "No," he said sarcastically.

"Apologize now!" Kate warned, pointing her finger at him.

Andrew smugly shook his head and drew up an evil grin. "She deserved it," he gloated.

Kate wanted to smack the look right off of his face. Her eyes briefly accepted his showdown-stare before turning to look at Megan, who watched them both with huge eyes.

"All she did was look at the fish," Kate said with all the authority she could muster.

Andrew shot his sister a dirty look. "Yeah, MY fish! And I don't want her looking at them," he hissed.

Kate turned from him without a response, grabbed his bag of clothes, and took them to the car along with her daughter. She started the heat so Megan wouldn't freeze, buckled her in, and walked back inside for Andrew.

"Let's go," Kate commanded.

Andrew glared at her through dark and distant eyes. "I already told you, I'm NOT going."

Kate's son had grown to be as tall as she, and had an extremely solid build. He stared at her as though he were sizing her up for a fight. Taking a step back, Kate decided to switch tactics fast before things got out of hand. "Go get in the car or I'm calling your father," she threatened.

"Go ahead," he dared her.

Kate reached into her pocket, pulled out a cell phone, and dialed Ed's work number. "I need you to talk with your son," she said when Ed answered the phone. "He waited until I drove forty minutes to get here in blizzard-like conditions and then tells me he's not coming."

Ed laughed, as though what he was hearing was funny. "Maybe he doesn't want to go with you," he chuckled.

"It's not funny," Kate yelled. "He hit his sister in the face a few minutes ago. I'm not putting up with this! What's been going on here to make him so angry?" she questioned, even though she knew her ex was never going to tell her what went on at his house.

"Nothing's been going on, Kate," he exploded. "Andrew's been perfectly fine. The problem is you don't know how to handle your own kid. No wonder he doesn't want to go with you."

Ed's heated response reminded Kate why she divorced him in the first place. "He probably doesn't want to come because he knows at my house he can't get away with everything like he does here," she told him. "Are you going to talk with him or not?"

"Fine, put him on," Ed grumbled.

Their conversation was quick, but whatever Ed said to him did the trick. Andrew hung up in a huff and turned to his mother. "Now are you happy?" he snipped.

"Ecstatic," Kate added. She picked up the Expo marker attached to the dry erase board on the fridge and scribbled Ed a note.

If his attitude doesn't change, he'll be back tomorrow.

Finally, after all the fighting, she managed to get him

into the car and headed home with both kids in tow.
Something she would regret for the rest of her life.

CHAPTER THREE

The deafening silence that stung the air was piercing. Andrew sat in the front seat of the car pouting miserably; headphones plugged his ears in an effort to pretend he was all alone in his world. The small talk his mother and sister tried to engage him in went unnoticed, and most of the ride home was spent in awkward quietness.

Heavy snow still fell outside, making it hard to discern their exact location. The wheels on the cherry-red SUV barely hugged the pavement as Kate carefully took each curve of the country road on their way home. She knew the roads like the back of her hand, but the blanket of white in front of them distorted where the road ended and the forest began. The only thing getting her through the treacherous drive was knowing her kids were together again.

Once Kate turned the vehicle into the cul-de-sac that led to the three-bedroom colonial she and her new husband, Joe Rose, bought after they married three years earlier, Andrew's attitude suddenly shifted. He chatted like a schoolboy as if the past forty minutes had never existed. The bipolar switch came out of thin air, but Kate was relieved with his friendlier attitude.

It was well past dinnertime when everyone walked through the front door, and the gurgling sounds of empty stomachs testified to it. Kate left Andrew's bags in the foyer along with all their snowy boots and headed straight to the kitchen to look for something quick to whip up as the kids got settled in. She reached into the cupboard, pulling out a box of spaghetti, a can of Prego sauce, and seasonings for the meatballs, then grabbed a large pot from the drawer below and filled it with water to boil. She was glad things had settled down with Andrew, and couldn't help but to smile as she heard the kids playing hide-and-seek together throughout the house. The sound of footsteps drifted from upstairs to down as the aroma of fresh meatballs began to fill the air.

When the pasta was al-dente, Kate fixed both kids a plate and set the food on the table. "Kids, dinner's done," she called up the second level where they were playing in the bedrooms.

Andrew flew downstairs with flushed cheeks, by-passed the dining room, and headed directly to the living room where he sat on the couch. Draping one arm along the back of the sofa, he rested the other along the armrest.

Megan emerged moments later, visible shaken as she walked into the kitchen. She looked up at her mother, eyes bulging as if she were in shock, and leaned into her mother's ear. "Andrew touched my butt," she whispered.

Breathless with disbelief, Kate glared out at Andrew who remained on the sofa, staring back at her with a deer-in–the-headlights look. She quickly turned away, scooped up Megan and rushed her into the downstairs bedroom so they were out of earshot of Andrew. She closed the door behind them, sat on the bed, and put Megan on her lap. "Honey, tell Mommy exactly what happened."

Megan looked scared to tattle on her brother again, but finally relented. "Andrew hurt me. He touched my butt," she repeated, and then as she often did because it was her autistic nature, tried to show what she meant by using body motions.

Kate's stomach curled as she witnessed her nine-year-old baby girl lying on her back with her legs up in the air, demonstrating the most obscene violation that could have ever been done to her.

Disgusted, she had to look away. From the corner of her eye Kate spotted a tiny brown tail sticking out from behind the laundry basket. Megan had brought her teddy bear, Chubbie, with her the night before when she climbed in bed with her mom in the middle of the night. How it got to the floor Kate wasn't sure, but she picked it up and handed it to her daughter. "Megan, I want you to stay in here with the door shut until I come back, then we'll talk some more. Do you understand?" she asked.

"Yes, Mommy," Megan said, taking the bear and hugging it tight against her chest.

Kate kissed her daughter's forehead then slipped out of the room to find Andrew, who had a lot of explaining to do. She grabbed him off the couch and ushered him into the den, slamming the door behind her. Kate's head spun so much she nearly passed out. She couldn't speak right away, for if she did, she knew she would have to face reality. For a moment, they stared at each other in complete silence. She didn't want to face the possibility her first-born child had abused his little sister.

When she finally summoned the courage to speak, she was quick and direct. "What did you do?" Kate demanded.

Andrew erased the scowl off his face in an attempt to look innocent. "Nothing. I didn't do anything," he replied in a trembling voice.

As much as she wanted his words to be true, Kate knew he was responsible for hurting his sister. The look on his face already told her he was guilty.

"Why?" was all she could muster. "Why would you do something like that...and to your little sister...why?"

Andrew continued to deny the accusation as he stood in front of his mother with a mixture of a cocky-attitude, and a look that revealed he had the fear of God in him at the same time. Yet, Kate still couldn't comprehend it. How could a twelve-year-old boy...her twelve-year-old son....do this to somebody? She was so numb she could barely bring herself to look at him.

My little girl's innocence had been taken away. She wanted to scream, slap his face, shake him...but she remained stoic-- afraid of what may happen if she allowed her true feelings to unleash. *I have to get him out of the house and away from Megan. Do I call the police and have them drag him off or call his father?* Calling Ed was the less mind-boggling choice.

"Don't move," she instructed Andrew as she walked back out to get the kitchen phone. Her fingers fumbled to dial the numbers. As she waited for her ex to pick up, her heart began to palpitate faster. After eight rings, she threw the phone down and started to cry. *How am I going to get Andrew out of the house?*

Shelly Mead, Ed's much younger girlfriend, only worked a few miles down the road. She and Kate got along pretty well, and truthfully, Kate felt better knowing there was a female figure to help watch over Andrew while he was with his father. She retrieved the phone from the floor, looked up Shelly's work number, and called her. While she waited for Shelly to pick up, she stared at her son who was still standing in the corner of the den. *Does he even care what happened to his sister?*

"Hello?" a voice answered after the sixth ring.

"Shelly, it's Kate. I need you to come get Andrew. He hurt Megan and has to go."

"Oh my gosh, what happened?" she gasped.

Kate shifted her weight and nervously began twirling strands of blonde hair around her finger. "I don't know the full story yet, but Megan told me he touched her butt. She's crying and Andrew is standing here looking smug. Can you come right now get him?"

"I'll be right there," Shelly promised.

Knowing somebody else was going to be with her helped to ease Kate's tension. She desperately needed support at the moment, even in the form of her ex-husbands new girlfriend. Shelly arrived within ten minutes, rushed into the house, and made a beeline in Andrew's direction. "How could you? She's your little sister, you pervert," she berated as if he was her own child.

Andrew stared at her, eyes nervously twitching.

"Don't move from your spot," Shelly ordered before coming back out to the living room to find Kate. "Do you mind if I take Megan upstairs so I can hear for myself what he did to her?"

"Go ahead," Kate answered without breaking her gaze from the family portrait that hung on the wall. Her two kids looked so young and innocent then. What she wouldn't give to be able to go back in time. "She's in the downstairs bedroom."

Shelly found Megan sitting on her mother's bed still playing with her teddy, and took her hand to walk her upstairs to her own room. Not wanting to be near Andrew, Kate walked out to the enclosed porch and watched him through the window as the sparkly snow fell out of the darkened sky. Her eyes burned, and she quickly sniffed back her vulnerability so she could go back inside with pride intact. She wouldn't show him her tears. He didn't deserve the satisfaction.

After what felt like an eternity, Shelly came back downstairs, dabbing her own eyes with a tissue. "I put a movie in for Megan and told her she could watch it upstairs while we talked," she told Kate.

"That was smart, thank you," she answered with a grateful smile.

"Listen, Megan told me the same thing she told you. Andrew really did touch her. I'm so sorry," Shelly said while offering Kate a consoling hug.

"I don't know what to do," Kate whispered as she briefly accepted Shelly's comforting embrace.

"I'll deal with Andrew," she said hugging her tighter. "You take care of Megan."

Turning away, Shelly walked toward Andrew and got in his face. Unlike Kate, she had no problems venting her anger. "Are you out of your mind? Why on earth would you do something like that? You're her big brother. You're supposed to be protecting her, not hurting her. Only a low-life would take advantage of a person with special needs. You're despicable!"

Andrew continued his silent, yet guilty stare.

Kate felt grateful Shelly was so angry because her own body remained in a state of shock and anger had not set in for her yet. When Shelly finished yelling at Andrew, she gave Kate another hug and told her she would call later in the night to check on Megan, then marched Andrew out to her car.

As Kate watched them drive away, her heart beat frantically with panic. *What does somebody do in this situation?* She knew she couldn't sit there and pretend nothing happened; she had to take action...but what?

There was no protocol for this type of situation. Not knowing what else to do, she called the pediatrician's after-hours number and paced the floor while the phone rang. When the answering service picked up, she couldn't find the words to tell them why she was calling. "My daughter...umm...was...umm...I need to speak with the doctor right away. It's an emergency."

"Ma'am, I need to know what the problem is," pressed the staff member.

"It's private," Kate answered, hoping it would be enough for her. "I really need to speak with the doctor."

"I will call the physician right away and have her get back to you," she said, evidently sensing the urgency. A few minutes later, the phone rang back. Through the tears and choked up words, Kate explained to the doctor what Andrew had done to Megan, and asked for guidance on what to do next.

"Where is he now?" Dr. Sanders asked calmly.

"I had somebody pick him up, he's no longer here," Kate whispered.

"Good," she asserted. "Now, it's very important you take Megan down to the emergency room to make sure there has not been any damage."

Dr. Sanders had been the kids' pediatrician their whole lives. Kate trusted her opinion, and always followed any advice she had given them. "Okay," she agreed, "we're going right now."

"Stay strong, Kate, and give Megan a hug for me," Dr. Sanders' voice sounded very empathetic as she spoke.

"I will," Kate replied and hung up the phone without even saying goodbye. She allowed herself a brief moment to catch her breath before attempting to move.

A million thoughts ran through her mind as she got their coats and boots on to leave. *How am I ever going to*

tell Joe my eldest child had sexually abused his little sister?
Joseph Rose was a very supportive husband, and had seen
Kate through some very tough times after she divorced Ed.
The man thrived on integrity, and knew how to treat a
woman well. Kate was lucky to have him her life.

Joe was due home from work any minute, but as
much as she needed him with her, there wasn't time to
wait. Frantically, she searched for a piece of paper, and
with a shaky hand, wrote a note before taking off.

We're at the hospital...please come!

They left dinner on the table untouched and climbed
into the car, slipping deep into the abyss of social
injustices yet to come.

CHAPTER FOUR

Kate's knees trembled as she and Megan entered the hospital through the automatic doors. The smell of alcohol instantly permeated their noses and Kate became lightheaded as they proceeded toward the registration desk. The receptionist was on the phone, so she quietly signed Megan in to be seen and found a seat for them in the waiting area. The room was filled with sick kids and injured adult, and she felt out of place next to them.

I want to go home. Megan needs me to be comforting her, not sitting at the emergency room.

Kate didn't want to be around anyone and wished she could take her daughter and find a quiet place where they could be by themselves. "Megan," the triage nurse called into the waiting room.

They both stood to walk into the next room as Kate's cell phone rang. Pulling it out of her purse, she noticed Joe's number on the caller ID. She needed him so badly to hold her hand and tell her everything would be okay, but didn't have the luxury of time. "I'll have to call you back," she said without a hello.

Joe wasn't going to be held off. "No, I need to know

what's going on, Kate. I came home from work and there's a note on the table saying you're at the hospital. What happened?"

She motioned Megan to sit in the chair next to the nurse, then turned her back and covered the phone with her hand in an attempt to camouflage what she said. "Andrew hurt Megan. I can't talk right now; the nurse is trying to ask me questions. I'll call you back."

"I'm getting in the car now to head over there. Call me on my cell as soon as you're done with the nurse." The concerned sound of Joe's voice was evident of his love for his family.

"I will," Kate sniffed back.

Joe loved his stepdaughter, and had proudly taken over raising her as his own child after he met Kate. "Is she going to be okay?" he asked. Not able to wrap her mind around the possibilities, Kate gently hung up the phone and put it back inside her purse.

Assuming Megan was sick, the triage nurse stuck a thermometer in her mouth and placed a blood pressure cuff on her arm. She marked off her vitals and then proceeded to ask about her medical history as she filled out a form. "What kind of symptoms is your daughter having tonight, Ma'am?"

Kate stared at her blankly, not knowing how she was going to bring herself to say the words again. "My daughter has been violated," was all she could manage to reply.

"What do you mean?" she inquired with a confused look on her face. Not having the strength to explain what she meant, Kate just stared at her.

"Did somebody touch your daughter?" the nurse asked in a hushed tone after closing the door so nobody could hear. Looking at her little girl, Kate slowly nodded yes.

"I'm going to take you to a private room so the doctors can exam her properly," she informed Kate, quickly guiding them down the hall away from the ER patients.

The two followed behind her slowly, neither wanting to go where they were headed. Their eyes diverted to the floor as they walked. The nurse stopped outside a door, gesturing out her arm for Kate and Megan to enter. Kate looked up and her heart nearly froze when she saw the OB-GYN sign outside the room.

The nurse had Megan sit on the bed and Kate's stomach turned as she noticed the stirrups at the end of it. She knew it would only be a matter of minutes before her little girl would have to use them. Trying to avoid it for as long as possible, Kate placed their coats on the chair, picked her daughter up and sat atop them. The triage nurse assured them it wouldn't be long before somebody would be in to take care of them, and then she disappeared. Kate didn't think she had the strength to go through this alone and wanted nothing more than to call Joe back. She leaned over and picked a book up from the counter, handed it to Megan to look at, and kissed her forehead before stepping outside the room. With each ring of the phone a new teardrop fell. One the third ring, her husband answered and she could no longer hold back the flow of tears.

"Hey..." Kate's voice trailed off and the only sound on the phone was one of a grieving mother.

"Kate, I'm almost there. Can you tell me what's going on now?"

"I think Andrew sexually abused Megan," she replied sullenly.

"What?" Joe exploded. "He raped his little sister? How

could he hurt her like that? He actually admitted to having sex with her?"

She ignored the vulgar words she so desperately didn't want to be true. "I don't know exactly what happened yet. All I know is she told me he touched her butt."

Knowing he would never let his wife or stepdaughter down in their time of need, Joe re-assured her. "It's going to be okay. I'm here for you both, Kate." Her swelling throat didn't allow for a response before hanging up. Megan needed her mother and she had to get back to her. Nothing else mattered.

When Kate returned to the room, she pulled two dolls out of the bag Megan had carried in from the car so she could play with them while they waited for the doctor to come in. She helped Megan comb their hair, and together they dressed them up for a pretend party. The dolls made small talk with each other and Kate was grateful for the diversion because she didn't know what to say to her daughter. There was nothing she could tell her to make her understand why they were in a hospital, and that she had done nothing wrong.

Kate kept the dolls playing long after Megan lost interest simply to occupy her own mind. She needed a distraction in order to stay strong and to ensure her daughter wouldn't see her cry.

A nurse with an understanding smile walked into the room and tousled Megan's long chestnut-blonde hair. "Hi sweetie, my name is Sara. I'm going to be helping you out tonight," she chatted as she began pulling shiny, sterile instruments out from different cupboards and drawers and lined them up on the counter in front of her. "Mom," she said turning to Kate, "I'm going to go to the pediatrics floor and find a gown small enough to fit Megan so she can change out of her clothes. I set a plastic bag on the counter. You will need to place her underwear in it so we can send it out for a DNA sample."

Sara sped out as swiftly as she had come. Neither Megan nor Kate had even acknowledged her presence. They sat in silence, Megan clinging tightly to her mother. Kate's mind wandered down the harrowing past, terrified she may have missed warning signs from her son that he had the capability to sexually abuse another person.

The nurse returned moments later with a tiny pink gown with teddy bears imprinted on it. Kate snapped back to the present as Sara handed it to her. Megan had no idea what the gown was for, but changed her clothes as she was told. Kate neatly folded up her jean skirt, tights, and Hello Kitty shirt, set them on top of their coats, and then helped Megan tie the cotton robe in the back. Carefully, she picked up her panties and placed them into the plastic bag, trying to ignore the eerie feeling of having to do so. Joe appeared at the doorway as she sealed it up.

"Comb your dolly's hair while Daddy and I talk," she told Megan who had sat on the doctor's medical stool and was spinning it in circles.

Joe and Kate stepped into the hallway--out of earshot, yet close enough where they could still see Megan. When her eyes met her husband's, the tears fell without her consent. He was the one person with whom Kate knew she could let her guard down. For a moment, she allowed herself to become vulnerable. While still unable to comprehend the complexity of it, Kate managed to fill Joe in on the few details of the abuse she knew. He pulled her in close and rested her head upon his shoulder so she could cry.

"I'm so sorry, Kate. Is Megan going to be okay?"

"The doctor hasn't examined her yet. I don't know."

Joe hugged his wife tight. He was as scared for his stepdaughter as his wife was. "Where is Andrew now?"

Kate lifted her head to meet her husband's eyes. "I called Shelly at work. She took him back to Ed's house."

"That little girl never did anything to anybody. Why would someone want to hurt her like that?" The fire in Joe's eyes started to rage. He would have done anything to protect Megan. "I'm going up there to give him a piece of my mind. I'll be back," he huffed and strode down the hall.

As he left, Kate ran after him. "Please don't leave right now, I really need you."

He thought for a moment. "You're right. If I went up there I'd probably end up killing the kid. I'm not about to go to jail because of the likes of him." The strength of their marriage went unspoken. They held each other tight and tried to regain their composures before heading back into the hospital room where they could turn their focus to Megan. She needed them both to be there for her more than anything.

"Knock, knock," Sarah called as she peeked her head back into the room. "I brought Dr. Ford with me to meet you, Megan. He's the nicest doctor at this hospital," she added. Kate couldn't help notice the rape kit she held in her hand.

"Nice to meet you, Megan," he greeted her. "Do you think you can be a big girl for me and hop up onto the bed?"

"I'll step out in the hallway," Joe told Kate, who grew pale as the nurse had Megan lay down in preparation for the exam. "You focus on keeping Megan calm."

Kate nodded as he left the room, then laced her fingers within her daughters and looked into her light brown eyes. "Everything's going to be okay. Mommy is here for you. The doctor needs to look down there to make sure you didn't get hurt," she cooed to her daughter.

Megan looked scared and confused, but nodded in agreement, as her tiny hand trembled inside of her mother's. Kate's heart ached for her. She had just experienced being sexually abused, and then her mother brings her to a place where they prodded around the same area that was violated. Megan had no comprehension what was going on and all Kate could do was tell her she was going to protect her.

Megan remained still during the exam, but her eyes begged her mother to make it all stop. Kate watched helplessly while her daughter lay on the bed spread-eagle, feet up in the stirrups. Seeing her in that position sent visions through Kate's head of her being abused. It was too much for any mother to witness, and Kate had to blink hard to fight back the salty tears that dripped onto her lips. The soft voice of the nurse comforting Megan echoed within the room as Kate's body and mind weaved in and out of awareness. Throughout the examination, the nurse distracted Megan with small talk while her mother softly caressed her cheek.

"Megan, you were so brave. The doctor is all done now and you can get dressed," Sara announced before she turned to Kate. "Mom, when you are done helping her, why don't you step outside the room and talk with me for a minute."

"Sure," Kate answered, even though all she wanted to do was scoop her daughter up and take her home. She slid Megan off the exam table and walked over to the counter to gather up her clothes. The white tights with dancing snowmen on them would have to double as panties. Her underwear was now considered evidence.

"You did a great job, Puddin'," Kate told Megan and placed a kiss on her forehead. "I'm sorry the doctor had to look down there, but we needed to know you weren't hurt."

Megan opened her mouth to respond, but a smile crept up on her face as her stepfather walked in the room waving a Hershey bar at her.

"Thanks, Dad!" she exclaimed, taking it out of his hands.

"Anytime, sweetie," he smiled giving her a hug. After helping her open the candy, Joe raised a curious eyebrow toward his wife, trying to find out how the exam went. Kate shook her head and mouthed that she didn't know the results yet.

Sara stuck her head back in the room. "Mrs. Rose, can I speak with you for a moment?" she asked. Kate glanced at Megan, not wanting to leave her daughter's side.

"Go. I'll keep her company," Joe assured his wife. Reluctantly, Kate stepped into the hall with the nurse.

"Mrs. Rose, we are mandated to call the authorities in situations like these. You will need to wait here until the police arrive so you can give a statement."

"A statement?" Kate echoed in a state of shock. "How am I going to tell them what happened when I don't know very much myself?"

"Tell them what you know; it's all you can do," Sara stated and headed out the door without another word.

As they waited, Joe and Kate took turns reading Megan stories to calm her down and then Kate softly rocked her in her arms as she sang off key. Megan found comfort in laying her head against her mother while she listened to the songs. "I'm hungry, Mama," she murmured as she curled up tighter onto Kate's lap.

"What do you want me to go get you?" Joe asked Megan. "Anything you want!"

Megan rested her chin in her hand, deep in thought.

"Chicken nuggets and fries," she told her daddy.

"Your favorite! I should have guessed," he teased as he stood to put his coat on. "And what do you think I should get for mom?"

"She always orders one of those yucky salads," she told him.

"Yeah she does," Joe agreed, teasingly scrunching up his face in disgust. "What kind of salad do you want, honey?"

Kate shook her head. "I don't want anything. I don't think I can stomach food right now."

He gave her a knowing half-smile then kissed them both goodbye. At ten o'clock, two police officers arrived at the hospital room; just moments after Joe left for McDonald's.

"Mrs. Rose?" one of the policemen called while knocking on the door as they both entered. "We received a call from the hospital about your daughter in reference to an abuse situation and we need to get a statement from you."

She gave a silent nod as she reached into her purse. "Give me a moment, please," Kate requested. She called Joe's cell phone to tell him the cops had just arrived, so there was no need for him to return to the hospital. They should be home shortly, and Megan could eat her food when they got there. When she hung up, the officers introduced themselves, then wasted no time in bombarding Kate with questions about her family. She supplied them with addresses and phone numbers for both Ed's and her households, and then explained the reason for the split custody between the two kids.

"Ma'am, can you step outside the room for a moment while we talk more about why you're here," one of the officers asked.

"Sure," she responded, relieved not to have to speak about the details in front of Megan. One officer followed her into the hall; the other sat in a chair next to Megan's bed. "Aren't you both coming out to speak with me?" Kate asked.

"He needs to question Megan separately. It's standard procedure, Ma'am," the first man assured. Kate knew the truth. They wanted to verify if their statements matched. Without a choice, she left her daughter in the hospital room with one of the policemen as she followed the other into the hallway.

The officer pulled out an affidavit and filled it out as Kate described the preceding events to him. He had so many questions it made her head spin. *Where were you when it happened? What did she tell you? Where is Andrew now? What about her biological father?*

When the officer finished speaking with Megan, he joined them in the hallway to question her mother about her mental ability. *What had Megan said? I hope she was able to convey what happened.* Kate explained Megan's autism diagnosis, and how it sometimes caused her trouble with verbal expression. She assured them Megan was able to give details to questions if they were asked in the right way. They had Kate sign her statement and explained they placed a hotline call to the Department of Social Services. Somebody would be contacting her to further investigate the case.

It was midnight before Megan was finally discharged from the hospital. Although Kate was wide awake, her body was exhausted after everything they had been through and only wanted to go home and get some sleep. She knew they had a long road ahead of them, and just wanted to crawl into bed and never come out.

As they drove out of the emergency room parking lot,

Kate noticed from the rearview mirror a police car had pulled out behind them as they merged onto the road. *It must be a coincidence. They have our statements.*

Kate drove home extra carefully. The police car took every turn she did, while keeping a safe distance behind her. After a few miles, the squad car made a left hand turn as Kate continued straight down the road to her home. She was relieved momentarily, until she drove by an empty parking lot and saw two more police vehicles sitting there. They pulled out as Kate drove past and started tailing her. Kate was so nervous she could barely drive.

Why are they following me? I brought my daughter down to the hospital where she was put through female hell; I gave the statements they had asked for. I did everything an honest citizen should have done in this situation. What reason did they have to follow me home when all we needed was peace and quiet?

By the time Kate entered her driveway, the police vehicles were right on her tail. She flinched as the reflection in the rearview mirror showed both cars had pulled in right behind her. *What is going on?* As Kate reached for the handle to open the door to get out, one of the officers approached her.

"We forgot to ask your daughter's birth date when we took your statement earlier."

I already gave you this information. It doesn't take three police cars to follow somebody home to ask something so trivial. Kate scooped up Megan from the backseat, where she was sound asleep in spite of the evening's events, and shouted her birth date at the officer as she headed toward the house.

"Thanks, that's all we needed," he called, as he climbed back into his car and pulled out behind his colleague.

Joe, who could hear voices coming from the driveway, met Kate on the front steps as the cops were leaving. He took Megan out of her arms and brought her in the house to tuck her in bed.

Scared, upset and confused, Kate trembled into the house and closed the door behind her. Her body slid down the back side and she wept uncontrollably the rest of the night.

CHAPTER FIVE

Morning came all too soon. Kate fought the urge to open her eyes as the sun shone through the window onto her tired face. The events of the previous evening raced through her mind, and she felt frozen in time.

Moments after she succumbed to the daylight, Megan wandered into her mother's room, Chubbie safely tucked away under her arm. Kate felt her daughter's small feet push against her back as she climbed in-between her mother and stepfather. As much as she longed to hold her daughter and let her know things would be all right, Kate found it hard to even look at her knowing her innocence had been ripped away, and she hadn't been able to protect her from it. The tears began to silently fall as she pretended to still be sleeping when Megan laid her head on the pillow along with her mother. Kate couldn't face her yet, and she felt awful because of it.

Joe sat up, stretched out his arms and let out a big yawn. "Who wants chocolate chip pancakes for breakfast?" he asked tiredly, sensing his wife needed more time before facing the world.

A small smile began to creep up on Megan's face.

"Chubbie and I do!" she squealed, tossing her bear up in the air and catching him on the way back down.

He put his fingers to his lips. "Ok, let's let Mommy sleep while you and me go make them," he whispered.

From the other room, Kate could hear her husband engage Megan in small talk as she ate her breakfast. She was so grateful, yet ashamed for needing a few more moments of calmness before she had to get up, and was forced to deal with the ramifications of what had unfolded the night before.

When Megan and Chubbie finished eating, Joe helped wash the sticky syrup off his stepdaughter's face, turned on the Disney Channel for her to watch, and went back into the bedroom to comfort his wife. "We'll get through this," he whispered in her ear as he sat next to her on the bed, rubbing her back as she buried her head within the pillow.

Kate turned over and bolted upright, her lips trembling with fear of the unknown. "Will we get through this? My daughter had to go through female hell yesterday, my son clearly committed some type of crime, and I have no idea what is going to become of our family."

Joe held her tight in his arms and let her cry on his shoulders as he rocked her back and forth. It was such a hard thing to comprehend and Kate's emotions were getting the best of her. Joe wiped her tears and looked her right in the eye. "Megan is the one who needs us right now. She's just a little girl who doesn't understand what happened to her last night and she needs somebody to be comforting her. You can't lie here all day and hide."

Kate knew her husband was right. *This isn't about me; it's about my daughter.* Attempting to find strength, she got out of bed and tied a robe around her.

"I'm proud of you, Kate," Joe told her. "It takes a

strong person to be able to stand back up after something like this. I'm going to get the shower started for you. Take your time, and come out renewed so you can put on a brave face for your daughter."

She managed a knowing smile before slipping away into the bathroom. The heat of the water felt Zen-like, and Kate allowed herself the luxury of letting the past twenty-four hours temporarily escape her mind. When the cold water began dripping from the shower head, Kate unwillingly turned off the knob and reached for a towel. She took her time dressing, attempting to savor the much needed calmness. Picking up her hairbrush off the vanity, she began rhythmically combing out her hair in long even strokes until the sound of the doorbell intrusively interrupted her cadence. *I don't want to see anybody right now. Maybe they'll leave if we pretend nobody's home.* Kate closed her eyes and tried to mentally will them away, but Joe had already opened the curtains in the living room to see who it was before she could protest.

"Honey, it looks like somebody who needs to talk with you," he warned.

"Who is it?" Kate moaned from the bedroom. "I don't want company right now."

Joe poked his head in the doorway to get his wife's attention. "I don't know, but you better get out here. I'm pretty sure it has something to do with last night."

As a school district employee, Kate knew Child Protective Services legally has twenty-four hours to make contact with the family in question after a hotline call is placed. They made no exception in this case. She was not ready to start dealing with legalities, but reluctantly went to the front door and opened it. A stout, impeccably dressed, older-looking woman holding a brief case stood before her.

"Hello. My name is Mrs. Jones, and I'm here to follow up on last night's visit to the emergency room. May I come in?" she asked while holding out a business card for Kate to take.

Joe, who stood behind his wife, reached out to accept the card. When Kate remained stoic, he gestured toward the kitchen table and pulled out a chair for their guest. Kate's muscles grew tense and lightheadedness set in as she watched Mrs. Jones reach into her brief case and pull out a file with her daughter's name on it. Joe pulled a chair out for his wife and Kate sat down across from their guest trying to appear attentive.

Mrs. Jones silently organized her paperwork before looking up at Kate and Joe. "Is Megan here? I'd like to talk with her as well."

Tilting her head, Kate gazed perplexedly at her. "She is, but she already gave a statement to the police last night. Mrs. Jones, Megan is autistic and doesn't fully understand what's going on. Can't we give her a little break this morning and just talk between us?"

Mrs. Jones didn't appear sympathetic to Megan's needs. "I'm sorry, Mrs. Rose, but it's my job to connect with the victim after a hotline call is placed. I will have to speak with her face-to-face."

"Fine," Kate relented, "I'll run upstairs and get her for you." She had no way of preparing Megan for what type of questions she may have to answer, and prayed the continued conversation about the abuse wouldn't traumatize her any further.

"Can I get you some coffee?" Joe offered.

Mrs. Jones politely declined "No, thank you," she said shaking her head. "I just need to speak with everyone then I'll be on my way."

"My stepdaughter is a very sweet girl," he began to

tell her, hoping to appeal to her senses. "She may have a disability, but that doesn't mean she can't distinguish between right and wrong. I know the authorities are pressed right now for answers, but you must realize she needs time to express herself."

Before she could respond, Kate and Megan made their way back to the kitchen. Kate pulled her daughter onto her lap and made introductions. "Megan, this is Mrs. Jones. She would like to ask you some questions. Can you say hello?"

"Hi," she whispered, avoiding eye contact.

Mrs. Jones greeted her with a handshake. "Hello, Megan. I was so sad when I heard you had to go to the hospital last night. Can you tell me what happened?"

Megan diverted her eyes to the floor, ignored the hand shake, and walked out to the living room. She began ritualistically lining up her Littlest Pet Shop toys in perfectly neat symmetrical rows along the carpet.

"Sorry," Kate apologized. "She sometimes struggles with new people. As you know, I brought her to the ER last night because her brother had inappropriately touched her. Her pediatrician suggested it was a good idea to make sure she didn't have any injuries from it."

"Where is her brother now?" Mrs. Jones asked with her notepad and pen in hand, ready to record every word.

"He's at his father's house. He only visits here on the weekends," Kate answered while nervously drumming her fingers on the table.

Mrs. Jones noted this in her notebook, using big letters and lots of underlines. "How come?" she pressed.

Joe placed a hand over his wife's to calm her fidgeting fingers as she summoned the courage to reveal her son's issues. "The past several years Andrew had been physically aggressive toward Megan. His psychologist suggested we separate them to keep her safe."

The rolling of her eyes clearly spoke the words that were obvious: Megan still wasn't safe, living with him or not. Setting down her pen, Mrs. Jones leaned in closer as she folded her arms across the table. "Do you have plans to have him back here?"

"No, I do not!" Kate exclaimed with a dismissive wave of the hand. "Not after what he's done."

"Very well," she said, closing up her notes. "It's my job to make sure Megan is safe right now. Here's the card of the woman who will be in charge of the ongoing investigation for your case. Her name is Mrs. Emmerson. She'll be in touch with you soon. Do you mind if I have a quick look around before I leave?"

Shaking her head, Kate watched as CPS canvassed every inch of the house. The proximity of the kids' bedrooms to one another appeared to be of great interest to her. When she was satisfied with her self-guided tour, Mrs. Jones made her way back to Joe and Kate. "Megan will be required to give a full statement to the investigator," she informed them. "It will be imperative to the case."

They quietly nodded in unison, and then Joe escorted Mrs. Jones out to the porch, closing the door behind her fast as she left. The tears Kate tried to hold back started to fall again, coupled with a head that pounded from anxiety. She knew this was only the beginning of the long road still ahead of them.

When Megan heard the door close, she wandered back into the kitchen and crawled onto her mother's lap. "I'm scared, Mommy," she admitted quietly, snuggling her head against her mother's chest.

Closing her arms tightly around her child, Kate cocooned her to make her feel safe. "Me too, honey."

"I'm scared of Andrew, and of Daddy-Ed," Megan added while briefly making eye contact with her mother.

Worry lines framed her mouth and tugged at her eyes. "You're scared of your father?" she asked, ensuring she enunciated each word so her daughter would clearly understand where the conversation was going.

Drawing nearer to her mother, Megan hid her face against Kate's chest. "Uh-huh," she nodded.

Praying in her mind Megan would say it was because he had yelled at her for something silly like spilling milk, but cautiously aware that it could be something far more serious, she took a casual approach to the question. "How come?"

"I just am," she grumbled and curled up on the fetal position. "I don't want to see either of them again."

Kate stroked the long strands of her daughter's hair that had fallen onto her lap. "I promise I'll keep you safe forever," she assured her. *Somehow, I will find a way to protect you.*

Joe, who had been listening to his stepdaughter talk with her mother, turned without a word and quietly slipped out of the room. Kate could hear him sniffling as he left, crying at the words his favorite little girl had just spoke.

The rest of the weekend was spent in a panic-stricken fog. Their bodies wavered between shock and sadness, without as much as a staggered breath between the two. Normalcy had disappeared. *What does somebody do after being sexually abused? How does life become normal again?* Kate didn't know how to explain to Megan why her brother would hurt her in such a way. Her disability left her with a trusting nature, and it was evident now more than ever it was a dangerous trait.

CHAPTER SIX

With grief encompassing her mind, Kate knew going back to her job right away was not an option. She had spent so much effort concentrating on her daughter that she hadn't dealt with the emotional toll the abuse had taken on her. While Joe had done an excellent job of trying to be there for both his wife and stepdaughter, she simply needed some alone time. By taking a week's worth of her available personal time, she could have a few hours each day while Megan was at school to try to sort through her feelings.

This time alone proved to be mentally too much for Kate. Without the distraction of being at work, the abuse took over every thought she had. She couldn't handle the strain her family was under and started to experience symptoms of a nervous breakdown. She'd get lost while driving and would have to pull over to think about where she was and which roads she needed to take to her destination, even though she had driven there a million times before. She would cry all day, couldn't eat, sleep, or remember the simplest of things. Her mind was reduced to a blank slate, leaving her void of any control she previously had.

One afternoon, Kate felt particularly overwhelmed and had been pacing the house aimlessly when she noticed Andrew's picture hanging on the wall. His dark eyes stared back at her and she lost all control. Like a switch, her body quickly shifted from the state of shock it had been in, to anger. Suddenly, she had the need to eliminate anything and everything of his. In a fit of hysteria, she rampaged through the house tearing down all the photos that contained her son and smashed them onto the floor, watching as the shattered glass flew everywhere.

Next, she grabbed his artwork off the fridge, rounded up all his toys, and threw them in a huge garbage bag. Seeing his things discarded like trash fueled her rage, and she headed up to his room to complete her mission. Kate tore the clothes out of his closet and dresser, slammed them into the growing bag, and threw it down the steps. By then her heart pounded with adrenaline as her eyes scoped out the next target—his bed. With a head full of steam, she ripped the sheets off, pausing long enough to wonder if he had ever done anything disgraceful on them, and then hurled the mattress over her head and down the stairs. The box spring soon followed.

The anger within Kate unleashed, her body ran on auto-pilot. She picked up Andrew's dresser and lunged it down the stairs, feeling a bit of satisfaction as each piece crashed down the steps and landed in a scattered heap at the bottom. The bed frame cut a hole in the wall as she tried to maneuver it around the corner to the staircase, but she didn't care. Kate continued forcing it until it fell. Joe, who had just come home on his lunch break, watched in horror as his wife cleared out the room in a crazy rage. He begged her to stop, but she couldn't. It was bringing her peace.

Mentally, she had to rid the house of Andrew's personal effects. If she was unable to look at anything that reminded her of the person who abused her daughter, how could she expect Megan to look at them? She didn't need a reminder of what had happened, and Kate had to help her move on.

Her pulse pumped hard; so enraged she couldn't stop. She continued the rampage until there was nothing left but four empty pale-blue walls in Andrew's bedroom. She stood still for a moment in the barren space, sweat dripping off her face as she bent over to try and catch her breath. The sound of her inhaling and exhaling echoed against the emptiness of the room. Gathering her second wind, she walked out and peered down the stairway that now held the remains of Andrew's belongings. They had to go. Climbing over the top of the fragments which lined nearly half the stairway, she carefully stepped around the pieces until she worked her way to the bottom. One by one, she hauled the broken furniture outside and heaved each piece into a snow bank, and continued with the rest of the house until there was nothing left of her son.

She had extinguished his existence, but not her memory.

CHAPTER SEVEN

"Hi, Kate," the receptionist at her doctor's office called out as she signed in. "Under the weather today? You don't look so hot." Kate squeezed out a half smile and handed her the insurance card and co-payment without a word. "The doc will get you fixed up in no time," said the receptionist after she printed out her receipt and handed Kate back her card. "Have a seat and the nurse will call you when they're ready."

"Thanks," she muttered. After the break down she had suffered the day before, Joe had convinced her she needed to see her primary care doctor to get herself stable before returning to work. Admittedly, she was scared for herself as well.

Kate slumped into an empty chair in the corner of the waiting area. There were kids on the other side of the room playing with toys. Typically, she enjoyed watching the little ones play, but with all the stress she had been under, she wanted the noise, and the world, to go away.

"Anyone sitting here?" an elderly lady asked pointing to the chair next to hers.

"No," Kate answered.

"You don't mind if I sit then, do you?"

Kate shook her head politely and wished she would leave her be.

The lady set her purse on the chair and started to take off her coat. "My name's Anna, but everyone calls me Gram."

"Kate," she responded with a nod. "Nice to meet you."

Anna smiled sweetly and pulled her wallet out of her purse after she sat. "These are my five grandkids. The youngest is only two. Isn't she sweet?" Anna held them up for Kate to admire.

"She is," Kate politely agreed.

Anna was eager to share about her life. "I was blessed with a large family. There was always someone around to keep an eye out for one another. Oh, when my children were little they would argue now and then, but when it came right down to it, they loved each other. Listen to me going on and on about myself. How about you? How many kids do you have?"

Sweat dripped down Kate's neck. *Do I lie and say Megan is an only child?* Pinpricks trickled up and down her arms as her breathing became heavier. Kate rocked back and forth to the rhythm of her breath trying to catch itself and she heard Anna call a nurse for help.

A brown paper bag was placed over Kate's face and she was led back into an exam room. As she got further away from Anna and her questions, the hyperventilating eased up.

"Nice slow breaths," the nurse reminded her. "The doctor will be in momentarily. I'm going to stay with you until he gets here."

"Thanks," Kate breathed into the bottom of the bag. "I

don't know what got into me."

"Whatever it was, it sure set you off," the nurse said.

Kate nodded in response, embarrassed about making such a scene. She was relieved when the doctor knocked on the door and the nurse left to tend to other patients.

"Hello, Kate," Dr. Cooper greeted without looking up from his chart. "How can I help you today?"

A single tear trickled down. Kate set the paper bag down on her lap and drew in a deep breath. "I need a few weeks off from work until I can better control my emotions. Can you write me an excuse?"

Dr. Cooper reached for a tissue and patted Kate's eyes. "What's going on?"

"My life is a mess," she sobbed. "Andrew hurt Megan. Really hurt her," she stressed, reaching for another tissue to dry her eyes again. During the process she accidently knocked over the stack of magazines next to her elbow. As they fell to the floor, she slunk further into her chair in sheer exasperation.

Dr. Cooper picked up the magazines, set them back on the counter, and put a hand on Kate's shoulder. "How did he hurt her?" he asked.

"He sexually abused her. Now the police and Child Protective Services are involved. The whole situation has got me frazzled. I can't stomach food anymore, I cry at the drop of a hat, I lay awake all night long staring at the ceiling, and during the day I can't concentrate on a single thing. I am literally losing my mind."

"Kate," Dr. Cooper interrupted. "Take a breath. I'm going to help you."

"You will?"

"Yes, but on one condition. I know a counselor who works with special needs children. She helps abuse victims work past their trauma. I will take you out of work for a couple of weeks if you agree to get Megan the help she needs, and if you also seek counseling for yourself."

Kate sighed, and nodded in agreement.

"Good," he confirmed. "I'll place a referral to the therapist for Megan. Now I am going to write you a prescription for Valium and some sleeping pills. These should help to calm you."

Taking the paperwork from him was like taking the weight of the world off Kate's shoulders. It was a little piece of grace in her ever chaotic life.

"Now you must also promise me you are not going to sit around dwelling on things," Dr. Cooper ordered. "Keeping yourself busy will be more productive."

"I'll try my best."

Dr. Cooper finished up his notations on her chart then stood and guided Kate toward check-out. "Great. Now go home and get some rest so you can take care of your daughter."

Kate exhaled and felt her stiff shoulders relax for the first time in days. On her way home she decided to do something special for Megan that night. Her sullen face had been haunting her mother for several days—perhaps her favorite meal would evoke a smile. Kate stopped at the grocery store and picked up fresh-ground hamburger, a loaf of warm Italian bread, and a jar of sauce. Megan's Italian heritage showed through her love of food from her ancestors' country.

When the school bus dropped Megan off that afternoon, Kate already had a stack of her favorite board games lined up and ready to play. She found if her daughter was preoccupied with something she enjoyed, it was easier for her to talk about her day. After an hour and six rounds of games later, Megan wore tired. "I'm hungry, Mama. Can we eat dinner now?" she asked.

"Daddy will be home soon, so we can start getting it ready. You set the table and I'll get the food going."

They both headed to the kitchen and began working on their assigned tasks. Aimlessly rolling the meatballs in her hand while the pasta boiled, it dawned on Kate the last time she prepared pasta, they never ate it. She drew in a deep breath to resist the flashbacks as a loud ringing interrupted her thoughts. Kate washed the residue off her hands and answered the phone.

The voice on the other end of the line was sweet and comforting. "Hello, my name is Ann Hart. I'm calling from Child Counseling and Psychological Services. Is this Kate Rose?"

"Yes," she replied. She knew Dr. Cooper placed the referral call, but hadn't expected to hear back from them so quickly.

"Hi, Kate. Your physician informed me about your daughter's recent trauma. I would like to offer you my assistance in helping your family."

We could use all the help we can get.

Not sure if Ann knew the extent of what had happened, Kate pressed for more. "Exactly what did Dr. Cooper tell you?"

"He told me your daughter has a disability and her older brother placed unwanted sexual advances on her. I want to assure you, Mrs. Rose, I am a Certified Professor of Child Psychotherapy and Play Therapy. I regularly work with children who have been abused as well as children who have special needs. Your daughter has been through a lot and needs someone to help her work through her feelings. I could assist her in doing this in a safe environment. This is the only way she will be able to move on in a healthy manner."

"I would appreciate anything you can do for her," Kate

replied honestly.

"Good. How does tomorrow morning sound? I can see her at nine o'clock."

"That sounds great. We'll see you then."

"I'm looking forward to meeting Megan," Ann answered sincerely. As Kate hung up the phone, she felt as though they were taking the first step towards recovery.

When Joe came home from work that evening, the table had already been set and the steam from the food had just started to wane. He hung his coat on the rack then placed a kiss on the top of Megan's head. "The table looks nice," he told her.

Megan beamed a proud smile. "Thanks, Daddy. I did it all by myself."

Joe grinned. "What's for dinner?"

"Spaghetti!" shrieked Megan as she sat in her chair, eager for the food to be served.

"Who wants to say grace?" Kate asked, bringing out the last of the food to be served.

"Me, me!" called Megan.

"Very well," she said. "Go ahead."

"Thank you for Mommy, and for Daddy, and for pasta that is so yummy in my tummy. The end," Megan declared. "Can we eat now?"

"Yes, we can eat," Kate laughed, passing her the bowl of spaghetti and tongs.

Joe giggled as Megan attempted to twirl her spaghetti onto the fork, but only managed to send a meatball flying to the floor.

"So, what's new around here today?" he asked.

"Well, I received a phone call from a play therapist named Ann. She thought it would be nice if I could bring Megan down to meet her tomorrow."

"She wants to meet me?" Megan asked with wide-eyes.

"Yes, she does. She wants to talk with you about what happened with Andrew."

"Oh," Megan groaned. "I don't like him anymore."

"I know you're mad, Megan, and that's why Ann wants to meet you. It's her job to talk with kids who are upset."

"Will you guys be there too?" she asked in-between bites.

"Daddy has to go to work, but I will be there in the waiting room with you. Only the kids are allowed to go in the back and play with her toys."

"She has toys?" Megan's eyes widened in surprise.

"Yes, she does. So what do you say? Would you like to meet her?"

A smile crept up on Megan's spaghetti-sauce face. "Okay," she grimaced, taking another bite of her Italian bread.

"Then it's settled," Joe piped in. "Tomorrow you will meet a new friend."

Megan made another attempt at twirling her pasta and Joe leaned over to kiss his wife's cheek. "She'll be fine," he whispered into her ear.

Megan did seem happy to meet a new friend, and Kate felt good about having her daughter talk with someone. She knew first hand that talking with her own best friend, Karen Davidson, had gotten her through a lot of tough times. Kate and Karen had been friends since the first grade. They'd seen one another through thick and thin over the years, and Kate wished Karen wasn't away visiting family right now. She needed her, just as much as she needed Joe, but hadn't wanted to break bad news to her about the investigation while she was on vacation. It would have to wait a few more days until she returned and they could talk privately, face-to-face.

***

Kate's eyes fluttered open at seven-thirty. Joe was getting ready for work and the sound of cartoons from the living room told her Megan was already up. Today was the day. The day Megan was to confront her fears and start rebuilding her life. Kate prayed she could do it.

They opened the door to Ann's office fifteen minutes early and walked into a large welcoming room. Books and toys lined the shelves under the windowsill. Newspaper clippings of Ann's achievements were posted on the wall; Professor, therapist, author, and counselor. Clearly, she was an expert in her field. The tension in Kate's body quickly diminished knowing Ann's knowledge could soon lead them all to a road of recovery.

A friendly receptionist called Kate over and handed her paperwork to fill out. She wrote a check to pay for the session, then sat against the wall where Megan played. Her nervousness led to her leg bouncing underneath the clipboard, causing her handwriting to become illegible on the intake forms. Anxiety crept back in with each question she had to answer. In order to keep her cool, she set them down, pulled Megan onto her lap, and read her a story.

A young woman with curly, chestnut-colored hair appeared from the back and greeted them with a smile so big any doubts Kate had quickly vanished. "Good morning!" Ann boomed as she walked toward them in the waiting room. "Is this my new friend Megan that I've heard so much about?"

"Do you have toys?" Megan asked.

"Why, yes I do," Ann assured her. "Would you like to see them?"

Megan nodded. Ann smiled and took her hand. "We'll be back soon, Mom," she assured, then led Megan through the double doors. Kate watched them disappear and wished she could go with them. Instead, she waited in a lonely chair out front and worried how Megan would respond to therapy. *What were they going to talk about?* As much as she wanted her daughter to forget what happened and put things behind her, she knew Ann was right. The only way for Megan to accomplish that was to deal with it head-on. Forty-five minutes after they had disappeared, Megan and Ann walked back out to the waiting room, hand in hand.

"Hi, Mommy," Megan called as she ran into Kate arms.

Kate scooped her up, and planted a big kiss on her cheek. "Hi, Puddin'. How'd it go?"

"We played with toys. Ann says I can come back again if I want. Can I, Mom?"

Kate set her daughter down and gestured for her to put her jacket on to leave. "Of course you can, honey," she said picking the book up from her chair she had been reading. "Can you put this back for me on that shelf over there after you get your coat zipped?"

With Megan out of earshot, Ann pulled Kate aside. "I want to assure you Megan did very well today. I promise I will keep you informed of all developments."

"I appreciate it."

"One more thing. Megan mentioned she is afraid of both her father and brother. She's not still seeing them is she?"

"No. I stopped all visitations the night she told me Andrew hurt her."

"Good. She needs to be separated from the negative in her life in order to move on."

"Will she be able to get past this?" Kate asked.

"The first step in helping Megan to move forward is to change things up. Since the attack happened in her bedroom, you may want to consider re-arranging the room, or perhaps putting a fresh new color of paint on the walls. Basically, anything to make it look and feel different, so every time she goes there she isn't reminded of what happened."

"That's a great idea. I'm willing to do anything I can to help her in the process. Thank you so much."

Ann offered Kate a hug before she headed over to help Megan put on her boots. Taking her daughter's tiny mitten-covered hand, Kate opened the door and they walked out into the bitter- cold air. This time when she breathed it in, Kate could only smell the freshness it offered.

"Let's stop off at the store and pick up some things to decorate your bedroom," Kate suggested to Megan once they were in the car.

"Can we look at the toys while we're there?"

"Anything you want, Puddin'," she replied while putting the keys into the ignition.

The project proved to be as beneficial to Kate as it was to Megan. It gave her a sense of direction and a positive way to focus her energy. With a can of petal-pink paint and coordinated glitter glaze in their cart, their mission was now to find as many frilly, girly, frou-frou items to blend in with the new walls.

They came upon sparkling curtain rods with feather boas, Disney Princess curtains with matching wall decals, and a fuzzy pink lamp to accessorize her room. A new princess comforter and bed skirt finalized the decor. It looked like something straight from the pages of her favorite *Pinkalicious* book.

Once home, they wasted no time in moving all of the furniture around and repainting the walls. By that evening her bedroom was unrecognizable. A vision Kate could only hope would transfer new thoughts into her daughter's head.

The next week when they saw Ann again, Megan was excited to tell her all about her new living quarters.

"How's it working?" Ann asked.

"I think it's helped for the most part, but we are still trying to deal with the night terrors and bed-wetting."

"Don't worry. We're not out of tricks yet," she winked. "This may sound silly, but here's what I want you to do. Fill a spray bottle with water along with a hint of glitter, and when you tuck her in at night, tell her it's magic fairy dust that makes all the bad stuff go away. It's similar to a dream catcher, but because you allow Megan to spray it herself, it's empowering her to take control of her own demons. The bed-wetting is psychosomatic. If we can control her fears, she'll be able to control her body functions."

"I'm willing to give it a try," Kate smiled with a tinge of hope.

That night, when she tucked Megan into bed, she read her a story and pulled out the secret weapon.

"Megan, I have something for you," Kate mentioned as she handed her the pretty pink bottle. "It's magic fairy dust to keep you safe. All you have to do is spray it in your room and nothing will hurt you while you are sleeping."

Megan scrunched up her tiny face and raised one eyebrow in a look of disbelief.

"Watch," Kate demonstrated as she squirted a dash in the air above her head. Tiny specks of glitter floated all over the room.

"Wow...let me try!" Megan pleaded.

Kate handed her the bottle and she joyfully sprayed

the entire room. Kate allowed her to have her fill of fun before turning out the lights. Megan slept so soundly that night they continued the charade for a whole month before they could finally wean it out of the nightly routine.

Ann was right: it was a magic potion.

CHAPTER EIGHT

March 2001

After the much-needed distraction of putting the final touches on redecorating Megan's room, the remainder of Kate's time off from work was spent trying to relax. Engrossing herself in books that previously served as dust collectors on her dresser, Kate temporarily escaped her life and entered into new worlds. It didn't seem to matter if *Chicken Soup* was warming her soul or if she escaped into a *Harlequin* getaway. As long as she was not sitting idle, her mind didn't care where she journeyed.

Snuggled on the couch with a hot bowl of popcorn on her lap and a new book in hand, Kate was deep into a mystery novel when the ringing phone interrupted her reading. "Kate, turn the television on to channel four," Karen instructed.

She had greatly missed having her friend by her side during all the turmoil, and was glad Karen had finally returned home. Karen's nervous voice prompted Kate to react without asking any questions. Finding the remote, she pressed the button and waited for the screen to focus.

She shifted her weight in anticipation as the sound of the day's breaking news filtered in from the local television station.

"In other news, a twelve-year-old boy is accused of sexually abusing a nine-year-old autistic girl. Because the children involved are minors, their names are being withheld for confidentiality, but sources say both the boy and his parents have been issued appearance tickets and will answer to the accusations in court in a few weeks."

Kate listened in horror as the television broadcasted her worst nightmare to the entire nation.

"Where did they get the story from?" Kate asked with staggered breaths.

"I don't know Kate, but you might want to close the curtains and lock the doors. You don't need any reporters trying to get the inside scoop of your family's tragedy. They've been running a continuous loop of the story every twenty minutes as part of the day's breaking news."

"I just want to crawl into a hole and die. I don't have the strength to deal with this."

"Yes, you do. I know it's hard, but your husband and I aren't going to let you do this by yourself. Go secure your house and when I get off work I'll take you and Megan out for dinner. I know tonight is Joe's late night at work, and there's no reason for you two to be sitting home alone."

"Thank you, Karen."

"You'd do the same for me. I'll see you later, Kate."

The rest of the day, Kate flipped through the television channels, watching to see which networks had broadcasted the dirty details of her life. Thankfully, the events surrounding the abuse were never publicly announced. Aside from the few people she told about the situation, nobody ever found out the nine-year-old girl in the news story was the victim of an incestuous relationship at the hands of her own brother.

"Who's ready for pizza?" Karen shouted as she walked through the door at five-thirty.

"I am. I am!" Megan chimed as she jumped into Karen's arms for a big bear hug.

"I'm going to order mine with anchovies," joked Karen.

"Eww. Gross!" cried Megan.

"More for me then," teased Karen as she set her goddaughter down and helped her get her shoes on. "I'll race you to the car."

"One, two, three, go," Megan yelled and took off for the garage. She climbed in the back seat and buckled her doll in next to her.

"How have you been holding up, Kate?" Karen asked as they pulled out of the driveway. "I feel horrible that I wasn't here to be with you."

"I'm better when I don't think about things. Can we change the subject please?"

"Sure," Karen conceded.

"What's new with you?" Kate asked.

"My brother had so much fun with me staying with him he said he'd be coming home for a visit next month. He's going to bring the whole family with him."

"How nice. It's been a while since he's been back here."

"Two years," Karen pointed out. "It'll be nice to have him home again."

"I don't want to see my brother," Megan piped in from the back seat. "He's bad. He licked me here and here," Megan disclosed while pointing to her genitals and breast. "I don't like that."

Karen slammed on the breaks. She turned toward her friend with a look of fear. Tears streamed down Kate's face as she reached back and grabbed Megan's hand. "I don't like that either honey. It was very wrong of him to touch you. Nobody is allowed to hurt you like that. I promise you I won't let it happen again." She hugged her mother's arm so tightly Kate didn't think she would ever let go.

Dinner and the car ride home was unusually quiet for three girls who were out on the town. There were no giggles, no smiles; simply a morose trio overcome by sadness.

After Kate tucked Megan into bed that night she returned downstairs a few minutes later, arms loaded with clothes she had taken out of her closet.

"What's this?" Kate asked as she dumped them on her lap.

"I don't want these anymore," Megan informed her.

Kate looked at the pile of clothes her daughter had discarded. Every skirt and pair of tights she owned was now trash to her.

"Honey, why don't you want these?"

"Because Andrew touched me when I wore a skirt. I don't want to wear one ever again. It scares me."

She scooped Megan onto her lap and cradled her in her arms. "Honey, what you were wearing had nothing to do with Andrew touching you."

"Then why did he do it?" she asked.

"I don't know," Kate replied honestly. "But I do know it had nothing to do with your clothes."

"Are you sure, Mommy?"

"Yes. That much I'm sure of," Kate told her. "Now how about putting these clothes back into your closet and I'll play a game of *Candy Land* with you."

"Okay," Megan said reluctantly.

Kate watched her scamper back upstairs and knew she had to do something to help her daughter break her mental connection between clothes and abuse. She headed to the phone and dialed Karen.

"Hello?"

"Hi, Karen."

"Kate, I'm so glad you called. I didn't want to talk in front of Megan. I'm so freaked out by what she said. When we spoke the other day you told me Andrew had touched her, but did you hear those details? The poor thing. I can't even imagine what she went through."

"It gets worse. She just emptied her closet out and wants to throw her clothes away because she thinks Andrew hurt her because of them."

"That's horrible!"

"I have to help her. Megan and I are going to have a rally day. Tomorrow we are going to put on our fanciest skirts, do our hair up nice and head to the mall for a girly day. I'm going to show her once and for all she doesn't need to be afraid to wear a dress because she was wearing one on the night of the attack. Will you join us? The more people she sees wearing skirts will only help to boost her confidence."

"Well, I don't usually wear skirts myself, but for Megan I'm willing to put one on. What time do you want to meet?"

"We'll see you there at noon," Kate said. The easy part was over. The hardest portion of her plan was to convince Megan to go along with it.

Trying to get her excitement up, Kate told her daughter they would be going to the mall the next day for shopping and lunch. Her intentions were to fill Megan's mind with fun, then slip her the skirt and tights as if nothing was out of the ordinary. She hoped she would be so distracted she wouldn't pick up on it.

When the sun rose the next morning, Kate laid out

Megan's best skirt and her old favorite tights with silver glitter splashed throughout. As soon as Megan saw them, her tiny face grew scared, eyes filling up with tears.

"I don't want to wear it," she said between sniffles.

"But it's skirt day at the mall! I've got one on and Karen is going to wear hers, too. We're all going to look beautiful and nothing is going to hurt us."

"Do I have to?" she asked meekly.

"I'm not going to force you, but I think it would be nice if you did."

Megan grabbed the weighted blanket her therapist gave her to use when her body needed calming, and draped it across her shoulders. She appeared to be contemplating what to do as she sat in silence.

"Just this once," she declared while marching off to change. Kate knew she wasn't buying her charade, but was grateful Megan at least attempted to appease her. She was about to embark on a mission to change the way her daughter viewed the world. If she could show her clothes would have no effect on how people treated her, she would have made a huge leap in her recovery.

They met Karen right on schedule and spent the day shopping and chatting up girl talk. Before they knew it, they had temporarily forgotten all their worries. Kate realized how long it had been since their world seemed normal. Each store they went in, they scoped out the fanciest dresses, using the changing rooms to have their own private fashion show. They never laughed so hard in their lives.

"Mommy, look at the beautiful dress hanging in the window," Megan exclaimed as they walked by Macy's. "Can I have it?"

Karen glanced at her friend with a gleam of hope in her eye.

"Of course you can Puddin'," Kate smirked, trying to hold back her excitement. "What color do you want it in?"

"Pink!" she shrieked.

Kate squeezed her hand and led her into the store with a spring in her step. Out of the corner of her eye, she caught Karen grinning from ear to ear.

CHAPTER NINE

The police keep calling. They had a crime and an exact location of their main suspect, yet they put the burden on Kate to produce the person who sexually abused her daughter. As she talked with them on the phone for the third time, Kate shook her head in disbelief. Their lack of motivation in this case didn't make sense.

"Ma'am, we need you to bring Andrew down to us so we can question him about the allegations," the deputy pressed.

"I gave you his address. Why can't you go to his house to talk to him?" Kate was really getting annoyed at their persistence.

"Ma'am, it would be easier if you brought him to us."

"Well, I'm not comfortable with doing that. I am not ready to face him. Plus, there is no way he's going to come with me willingly after what's happened."

"Ma'am, if you pick him up from school and drive him down here we can get his statement and move on with the case."

"So in his mind I'm the bad guy because I brought him

down to the police station. No way!" *Why can't they drive up there themselves...isn't that their job?* "If a stranger had raped my daughter would you still expect me to have to be responsible for finding him? It isn't right."

"Mrs. Rose, tomorrow a detective will be waiting to talk with your son at noon. Pick him up from school without your ex-husband knowing and bring him down to the station," he badgered.

Kate was in a quandary. She wanted justice for her little girl, yet at the same time, was nauseous at the thought of seeing the person who had defiled her. She didn't feel it was her responsibility to assure the police got a statement, and resented how they put the demands on her shoulders. Tired of feeling bullied, Kate relented. "I'll do it," she told him in a quiet voice. "We'll be there at noon."

"Detective Hite will be waiting for you. See you then," he said then hung up without another word.

Kate clicked the off button on the phone and immediately turned it back on to call Joe at work.

"Can you take tomorrow off? I need you to come with me to the police station."

"What's going on, Kate?"

"The police are forcing me to bring Andrew down to them for questioning."

"Why on earth would you agree to it? It's their job to find him, not yours."

"I know it is, but they won't go get him themselves. They were very persistent. I only agreed out of sheer exhaustion. Plus, if it helps Megan get vindication, then it will be worth it."

"Don't worry, I'll drive you there. I don't want you alone with Andrew anyway."

"Thanks, Joe. We'll talk more about it when you get

home."

"Okay honey, see you soon."

To keep busy, Kate took to the family room and organized the shelves that were already in perfect order. By the time Joe came home from work, she had rearranged the furniture three times. She knew if she kept still, she'd go stir crazy.

***

The alarm clock went off at seven that morning. Kate drew the covers over her head and ignored the buzzing sound that rang into her ears. She wasn't ready for what she had to do.

Joe got Megan ready for school and hugged her goodbye when the bus pulled up to the house. When it had disappeared down the street, he came into the bedroom and pulled the blankets off his wife.

"It's time," he announced.

With a groan, Kate slowly rose and headed toward the shower. Joe had the car warmed up by the time she was dressed and helped her put on a coat and as whispered in her ear. "We're in this together."

She wanted to vomit the entire ride up to Andrew's school. Kate hadn't been able to bring herself to speak with him since he attacked his sister, and emotionally she still wasn't ready to face him. *Why did you violate your sister's trust? You should be protecting her, not hurting her. Where did you learn such repulsive acts?* These questions were unsettling, yet endless within her.

As Joe pulled into the crowded school parking lot, he could sense the nervousness in his wife. He kissed her cheek and told her how proud he was at her bravery. Kate wasn't sure if it was valor or cowardice, but more of a force that guided her inside the building alone. Her legs shook so much she could barely get out of the car to make the short walk into the school. Through the disorientation, she found the main office and managed to tell the secretaries she needed to sign her child out for an appointment. Doing so made her realize how hard it was to say those words...*her child.*

It couldn't be *her child* who had done such vile things against her daughter. It certainly wasn't *her child* who was about to be taken down to the police station to be interrogated by detectives. Kate's body shivered thinking about it. Was he her child anymore?

Unsure if Ed had put her name on the school paperwork under those allowed to pick up Andrew from the building when he registered him in the new district, Kate held her breath as the secretary checked in Andrew's file to verify if her name was listed. She only took a sip of air after they offered her a seat while they called Andrew's classroom for him. Kate politely smiled and sat in one of the blue chairs to wait while he gathered up his belongings. Her stomach knotted up instantly. Andrew had not been expecting anyone.

What if he puts up a stink at the school? He could tell the office personnel he doesn't want to leave with me...then what? It was a very real possibility considering the situation. Even the hardest criminal would have a hard time facing his mom after committing such acts. *What would I do if he refused to come?* She had no backup plan. If she didn't sign him out, there would be no other way to get him to the police station to be questioned.

After ten painful minutes, Andrew's figure slowly emerged from down the hallway. Kate grew dizzy as he walked closer. From the distance, she noticed he appeared rattled at the sight of his mother. She was grateful, hoping it was a sign he might be ashamed of his actions. Kate diverted her eyes from him as he approached and thanked the secretaries before turning toward the door. They didn't speak a word as Andrew followed her out of the school and into the parking lot. She was surprised when he hopped into the car without a single question.

Kate's hands shook as she opened the passenger side door to get in, and they continued to tremble during the half-hour drive back to the police barracks. She thanked God for the love of her husband for trying to make small talk with Andrew to ease the awkwardness of the situation. She didn't want to be sitting this close to the person who stole her daughter's innocence, nor could she stomach the thought of looking at him. Yet, she also felt like a traitor for taking her first-born child to the authorities to gain information to prove he had indeed committed a heinous crime.

As Joe pulled the car into the police parking lot, Kate breathed a small sigh of relief. She needed to distance herself from Andrew. She didn't dare look at his reaction when he realized where they were, but was mentally prepared for him to make a run for it. As she stepped out of the car, her breakfast made its way back up into her throat. Somehow, she managed to swallow it back as the three of them slowly walked inside the Public Safety Building.

Joe informed the person at the front desk of their appointment and he escorted the trio in. Detective Hite was already waiting for Andrew once they got beyond the metal detectors, and he asked Joe and Kate to sit in the waiting room while he spoke with Andrew alone. Kate watched her son walk down the hall with the police officer. As soon as they were out of sight, her emotions took over. Needing to be alone, she ran into the bathroom, vomited and cried.

When she was composed enough to face Joe again, slowly she walked out and joined him in the empty rows of chairs. Neither of them knew what to expect from all this, yet was aware the outcome could be detrimental. Kate paced up and down the hallways until the officer re-appeared an hour and a half later with Andrew sulking behind him.

"Mrs. Rose, I need to speak with you alone," Detective Hite said. Slowly, she stood as Andrew made his way toward the restroom. "Keep an eye on him," the officer warned Joe. "Don't let him out of your sight!"

That was her first clue things were about to get serious. Cautiously, Kate followed the detective into a small, stuffy questioning room. It reeked of poor choices and guilty consciences. Her stomach knotted.

"Mrs. Rose," he began with a serious face. "Andrew has made graphic confessions. I need you to listen as I read the deposition back to him, recapping everything he has confessed to."

She gulped. Any doubts that lingered in her mind about Andrew's innocence vanished on the spot.

"I'm warning you now. You are about to hear a lot of sexual details. It's very important you keep a straight face while listening to the confession. No matter what your initial response is, don't make any comments or show him you are uncomfortable. If you do, we run the risk that Andrew may rescind his statement."

Sweat poured down her face as she clutched her purse close to her chest. The sound of her heart pounding echoed into her ears. *Not respond? How did he expect me to sit as if nothing has happened while my child divulges his sexual interludes?*

The officer sensed her lack of confidence to withhold emotions and tried appealing to her motherly instincts.

"This may be Andrew's only chance to get some much needed help. If he gets into the justice system, he will be mandated to receive therapy suited to his needs."

Dr. Covington's words came flooding back to her. *"One day he's going to do something that will land him at the mercy of the court system. My best guess is he won't get the level of help he truly needs until then."*

As much as Kate knew Andrew needed an intervention, she wasn't sure she could listen passively without having a reaction. "I understand," was all she could muster.

"Good. I'll go get Andrew and be right back."

As soon as he left, reality hit. No longer would Kate have any more questions, any more doubts. Her daughter's abuser was going to sit across from her and admit the dirty details of his crime. Her head dropped between her legs as her breath rapidly increased. When the sound of footsteps got closer, she knew she needed a way to calm herself, so she grabbed a Koosh ball from a nearby bin and sat upright. She clinched the slippery rubber tight within her fist and felt a release of anxiety. Her skills as an actress were about to be tested.

Moments later the door open. Andrew and the officer sat across from her. Immediately, Kate diverted her vision to the wall opposite of them.

"What I have in front of me is a written record of the statements Andrew has willingly provided to me," the detective began. "I am going to read the document aloud to ensure this is indeed what Andrew wants to say and then both of you will need to sign it. Does everyone understand?"

Everyone nodded in agreement. As the words began, Kate's whole body began to tremble. Sordid confessions from the person who used to be her child were revealed.

Now, instead of her son, she sat across from a rapist.

Kate was so confused she actually slipped in and out of consciousness as the statement was being read. She heard phrases such as, "At my dad's house I used to get a hard on when I would see Megan come out of the bathroom naked after her bath."

She used to come out naked to go to her room to get dressed? Why wouldn't her father make sure she had her pajamas with her in the bathroom? Why on earth was she walking around naked? The questions raced through Kate's head. Just when she thought things couldn't get any worse, the officer continued reading Andrew's statement.

"I held her down and took off her clothes. I asked her to touch me but she said gross. I licked and petted her."

The horrifying phrases kept coming. Kate couldn't believe the things her baby girl had endured, nor could she even begin to imagine what she had been thinking or feeling at the time. She must have been so scared. Kate's heart skipped another beat as the conversation took an unexpected ugly turn.

Megan had not been Andrew's only victim.

For the past year and a half, Andrew had been abusing Shelly's four-year-old son, T.J. The officer continued reading the deposition without a single waver in his voice. The details went on and on. As they resonated, Kate's head spun into dizziness. She sat there, stunned. Her expression remained stoic and frozen as she had been instructed, but her body was frozen as well. She honestly didn't know how to react and went into a state of shock as she was forced to listen to all of the monstrosities. Kate could not believe the things this twelve-year-old child, her first-born son, was confessing. A baby was describing actions most adults couldn't even fathom. She needed to know how he had learned about such things, and worse yet, how long had he been doing them to other people.

It felt like an eternity until all of the details of the crime had been read. Kate watched as Andrew signed the affidavit and she was asked to sign her name below as a witness. "Mrs. Rose, with the confession Andrew has provided us, he will be issued a ticket for sexual abuse, then booked for the crime. Because of his age, he will immediately be released on his own recognizance. However, it is state law if a child is being charged with a crime, an adult also needs to be charged as the responsible person. I want you to go call Andrew's father and have him come down here. We're going to issue him the ticket instead of you before releasing Andrew back to his care. Then you're free to go."

Kate made her way out to the waiting room to find Joe, then picked up her cell phone to call her ex-husband. Her mind scrambled to think of a way to express the words no parent ever thought he or she would have to say.

"You need to come down to the police station. They're arresting Andrew."

"For what?" Ed exploded.

"Sexual abuse," she informed him. Kate left out the part about him being issued an appearance ticket as well, and then hung up the phone as fast as she could so he didn't have time to ask any questions.

Joe put his arms around his wife's shoulder and escorted her to the car. Three went to the police station that day, only two walked out. Kate went home and cried any remaining tears she had left within her.

In the days following the confession, Kate couldn't stop thinking about how Andrew assaulted T.J., and wondered how their family was dealing with this. She started to grieve for him, and thought about how if it had not been for Megan being so naïve and not realizing there would be consequences if she told, the abuse might still be happening to him. For once, Kate was glad Megan didn't fully mentally understand cause and effect, because it meant she had saved another child from further abuse.

She was a hero in disguise.

Kate's mind became overwhelmed thinking how her own son had hurt that little boy. She became very sad for his family, and was compelled to contact Shelly and offer a belated apology and shoulder to cry on as her family started to figure out for themselves how to heal. She couldn't feel anything for Andrew, but cried for the people he had hurt.

Shame came over Kate to think she had birthed such a monster. Guilt rushed through her body for not being aware of what was going on to prevent it in the first place. Sadly, the truth was she didn't know, nor had ever seen any signs of him being sexually abusive. Her only concerns had been for his physical aggressions. Never in her wildest dreams would she have anticipated sexual abuse.

It was then Kate started to mourn the loss of her son. She grieved as if he had passed...for part of him had died within her. The trusting, unconditional love was gone. All that was left now were the remains of somebody she no longer recognized, somebody she would never understand. From that point on, Kate buried the memories of her son.

CHAPTER TEN

Just when Kate thought she could start piecing her life back together, the notion was shattered by another call from Child Protective Services.

"Mrs. Rose, it's Mrs. Emmerson from CPS. I believe Mrs. Jones told you I would be calling to investigate the case. How is your family doing?"

"We're trying to hold it together," she answered pensively. "Is there something I can help you with?"

"We need to conduct an interview with Megan. There are lapses in the testimony she gave to the police at the hospital, and now that she's had time to digest things, we are hoping she could give us a detailed timeline of events. It will really help to validate her story."

"Validate her story? Are you saying you don't believe her?"

"Please don't take offense. From a legal standpoint, we need something concrete to go on. Tomorrow, Detective Hite and I would like to stop by and talk with her."

"But she can't fully express herself," Kate's voice trailed off; the conclusion was inescapable.

"She is capable of speaking, isn't she?"

"Yes she is, but she can't give detailed explanations. Everything is black and white to her. There's no gray area in her world."

"I would like to hear what Megan has to say. Will nine-thirty tomorrow morning work for you?"

"That will be fine," Kate relented with a sigh. "I'll keep her home from school." She hung up the phone and ran to her filing cabinet, throwing folder upon folder on the floor until she found the one marked school papers. She flipped through the old report cards and art paintings until she found a copy of Megan's Individual Education Plan (IEP)-- the twenty-two-page legal document contained some glimmer of hope.

Kate took a highlighter and marked off sections within the paperwork that stated how Megan needed to have questions asked. Who, what, and where questions were tricky for her—open-ended questions even harder. She flagged the parts of the document that specified how Megan needed to have questions presented in simplified language and provided with a few choices for the answer. Having options for her to choose from were crucial in getting a valid response.

Knowing she needed this kind of questioning worried Kate. She knew CPS was not allowed to prompt the child in any way. Their job was to ask what happened and Megan would be expected to give an answer.

After she scrutinized the last page, she set the IEP on the counter and drummed her fingers on top of it. Lightly at first, then harder and harder. The more she stared at the paperwork, the more anxious she became.

Grabbing a sponge, Kate began to scrub the counters,

the walls, the appliances. Her nervous energy grew. The floors were mopped, cupboards dusted, dishes rearranged. She couldn't sit still. The harder she cleaned, the faster her heart beat. The nervous energy needed a release.

Kate didn't even feel the pain as she reached into the steamy bucket of bleach. Down on all fours, she scrubbed until blood dripped from her raw hands onto the shiny floor. She stretched out to clean it up, paused at her reflection from the wax, and slumped to the floor in exhaustion.

I need to get out of this house before I totally lose my mind.

Kate wrapped gauze around her wounds, changed her clothes, and grabbed the car keys. The car seemed to be on auto-pilot as she entered the Public Safety Center parking lot. *Why am I here? I'm sure the judge will issue an Order of Protection for Megan at Andrew's upcoming court appearance. Won't he?*

She was not willing to take Megan's safety for granted. Kate picked her purse off the car seat, walked inside the building, and requested the paperwork for a protective order from the clerk. She handed over the forms and explained that Kate would be notified of the court date after the papers were processed. She filled them out, then drove home.

The next morning, Mrs. Emmerson from Child Protective Services and Detective Hite from the sheriff's office showed up at Kate's door, right on schedule. The detective sat down at the table when Mrs. Emmerson asked Megan if she could see her bedroom. Megan took her upstairs to show off all her toys. As soon as they were out of earshot, the detective began questioning Kate.

"Mrs. Rose, where were you when the alleged abuse

happened?"

Kate's mind circled back to that night, wishing she could somehow alter the past so it would have never happened. "I was in the kitchen cooking dinner. The kids were playing hide-and-seek around the house."

He wrote down Kate's statement in his notepad. "Where you watching them at all?"

"Of course I was watching them. They were going from room to room hiding. I saw them every time one came by to find a new hiding spot."

"And when did your daughter tell you her brother had hurt her?"

"They had been playing for about thirty-minutes. I had just taken the spaghetti off the stove when she came and told me."

"And does your daughter tell a lot of stories?"

Her eyes widened in disbelief at his words. "My daughter doesn't tell any stories," she clarified. "I wish she knew how to but her mind doesn't work that way."

Detective Hite ignored the fact she had raised her voice at him and continued with his questioning. "What exactly is your daughter's disability?"

"She's autistic, Mr. Hite," Kate blurted out in a not-so-nice tone. "Kids of her caliber don't make up stories, they repeat the facts."

She handed him Megan's IEP in hopes he would understand their normal questioning tactics might need to be altered. He looked at it briefly then set it down just as Megan and Mrs. Emmerson re-appeared and joined them at the table. Detective Hite drew out the chair next to him for Megan. Kate sat quietly while he questioned her, only gesturing to Mrs. Emmerson to take a look at the IEP the detective had set aside.

"Was your brother over to visit you recently?"

Detective Hite asked.

Megan looked down to the ground. "Yes," she quietly answered.

"Is there anything you want to tell me about the visit?"

Megan shook her head no. Kate reminded Detective Hite he would need to be more direct with his questioning. He looked displeased at the interruption, and continued with an irritating tone. "Did your brother touch you?"

Megan curled her knees up to her chest and hunched over as she nodded yes.

"Where?" he asked.

She pointed to her pants, then hid her face in the corner of her elbow. "Honey, you need to tell him if Andrew touched you on the outside of your pants or on the inside," Kate interjected.

"On the inside," Megan answered quietly.

Mrs. Emmerson looked miffed. "Mrs. Rose, can you sit next to me so we can go over her IEP?"

Kate knew they thought she was interfering with the questioning, but she had to be sure they got all the information they needed. If they couldn't ask Megan in a manner she understood, then she needed to ensure her daughter was able to verbalize what had happened to her.

"Here are the names and numbers of Megan's special education teacher and speech teacher," Kate offered, handing a copy to both Detective Hite and Mrs. Emmerson. "They will be able to concur with Megan's abilities and discuss what strategies they use while conversing with her."

"Not necessary," Mrs. Emmerson snipped, pushing the paper back.

"Please," Kate begged. "I know how important my daughter's statements are. Don't dismiss her because her answers have been vague."

"We have all we need for now," Detective Hite said. "We'll give our findings to the judge before the court date."

They walked out and whispered to one another before getting in their car to leave. All Kate could do was wait.

CHAPTER ELEVEN

April 2001

Kate's twitching hands could barely button her silk shirt as she got dressed. Joe gently took them within his and kissed the tip of her nose. Leaning his forehead toward her, he pressed his body against her until she calmed. Once she relaxed, Joe took her buttons and slid each one inside the slits and smoothed out the creases on her shirt to make her look presentable.

"Are you ready to go?" he asked.

"No."

"It's going to be okay, Kate," Joe tried to reassure. "Andrew's case will only be presented to the judge today. No decision will be made."

"I know, but both of my children's futures are hanging in the balance," she pointed out.

"Do you know how proud I am of you right now? You have been through hell and yet here you are still standing up for your kids."

"I guess," Kate dismissed, not seeing it as anything any mother wouldn't do for her children.

"That kind of strength isn't easy. I admire you."

She wrapped her arms around her husband's neck. "Thanks, Joe. You always have been my rock."

Pulling up next to the brick building, Kate tried to put on a brave face for her husband, though it was a thinly-veiled façade. She wasn't sure if she could handle the outcome. They entered through the court room doors in dead silence.

It was odd being there for both the prosecution and the defense. As they walked into the courtroom, Kate hesitated for a moment. Two tables were strategically placed in front of them. Kate wasn't sure which side to sit on, as she was playing a double role as the mother of a child who had been victimized *and* the mother of a child who had been accused of horrendous crimes. Right there, she was being forced to choose between the two kids, a situation no mother ever wants to be in.

She glanced back and forth knowing whichever decision she made would set the tone for the rest of her life. Where was her loyalty going to lie?

Joe nudged Kate toward the prosecution side and she followed behind feeling as if she had just betrayed her eldest. She looked at all the strange faces there. On the defense side were the District Attorney, the Family Court Attorney, and of course Andrew and Ed. On the prosecution side were Child Protective Services, the Department of Social Services, along with Joe and Kate.

"All rise. The honorable Judge Lagoe, presiding."

Everyone listened as the judge read off the accusations and the court reporter feverishly typed every word. "Upon information and belief, in or about the month of February, the Respondent did knowingly act in a manner likely to be injurious to the physical, mental, or moral welfare of a child less than seventeen years old. Respondent did knowingly engage in hand to breast, hand to vagina, and mouth to breast contact with his sister, Megan. This act, if had been committed by an adult, would constitute the crime of Sexual Abuse in the First Degree, a Class D Felony as well as Endangering the Welfare of a Child, a Class A Misdemeanor."

"Furthermore, the Respondent did intentionally and unlawfully engage in hand to penis, mouth to penis, and penis to penis contact with an unrelated child under the age of five years old. If committed by an adult this would constitute as Sexual Abuse in the First Degree, a Class D Felony. In addition, the Respondent is charged with mouth to penis contact on more than one occasion, which, if committed by an adult, would constitute the crime of Criminal Sexual Act in the First Degree, a Class B Felony."

Ed sat next to his son at the table, neither one showing any signs of remorse.

"Andrew, do you understand the charges the state has brought against you?"

He stood and muttered a meek "yes" without making eye contact with the judge.

"How do you plea?" the judge asked.

"Not guilty."

"Your honor," interrupted the Family Court Attorney. "I would like to request an adjournment on the case so we can have time to gather information for the defense,"

"Very well. We will reconvene in three weeks. In the meantime, I am ordering a restraining order against Andrew. He is to have no contact with his victim, T.J., and is to have no unsupervised contact with any child under the age of sixteen."

"Your honor," Kate piped up, "Will there be a protection order for Megan as well?"

"The motion for the Order of Protection filed on Megan's behalf is hereby denied. Furthermore, any visitation either parent has with Megan is to coincide with their visitations with Andrew."

"Your honor, I don't understand," she broke in again. "Megan being victimized was no different than what happened to T.J., why isn't she entitled to a Protection Order and he is?"

"Because they are brother and sister, and they need to be together. The children will be supervised by whichever parent they are with."

"But your honor..."

"End of discussion, Mrs. Rose," Judge Lagoe ordered. Just like that, it had been decided. Megan did not deserve to be protected in his eyes. She was Andrew's little sister and nothing was going to interfere with the sibling relationship. Not even incest.

Infuriated, Kate couldn't hold back. "Your honor," she blurted out. "The defendant confessed to sexually abusing my daughter. I don't understand why the court is unwilling to give her an Order of Protection because they are related. Are you saying it's okay to rape somebody if you're a blood relative? T.J. received a protection order without his family even applying for one. It was given solely because a crime was committed against him. The crime against Megan was no different and it should be treated as such."

"Mrs. Rose, my decision is final. There will be no restraining order. I will however err on the side of caution until your next court date. The original visitation agreement is hereby vacated. From here on out Megan is to visit with her father on every other Saturday night, while Andrew is to visit with his mother during the same time. Both parents are expected to make certain the kids are kept separate during these visitations."

I wish he would order Megan to be released from all

visitations with her father. I feel like I am letting her down once again.

"Andrew is to receive a sexual offender evaluation before returning back to this court so we can proceed with the charges. Both parents will be required to pay for half of the initial evaluation."

Kate's jaw dropped. *Did the judge just require me to pay for Megan's offender? If any other person had abused my daughter, I would not be responsible to get help for them. I'm the only one paying for Megan's therapy. Why does Ed get away with not having full responsibility for anything?*

"The court assigns Mr. Fox as law guardian to both of the children. I encourage each parent to seek council as well. Since all interested parties have not had a chance to fully interview the children, we are adjourned for the day."

As they left the courtroom, the spectators glanced at Kate with pity. When her and Joe were the only ones left, she blotted the tears from her eyes and opened a compact to fix her makeup. She didn't recognize the person looking back. *Who am I? Am I the mother of a little girl who was subjected to a horrific experience, or am I simply a woman who bore a demon?*

She closed the mirror, rose to her feet, and made her way out the courtroom door. Kate hung her head low knowing she would not be able to follow through with bringing Andrew back into her house. She needed time away from him to figure out who he was, and who she was to him.

***

Several weeks after the hearing, she hit her breaking point. There were still so many questions burning in her mind; questions only Andrew would be able to answer.

Kate needed to start piecing her life back together, and for that to happen, she would have to talk to her son.

Each time she considered speaking with Andrew, her heart felt like it was being torn in two. Everyone from family to therapists pressured her to reunite with him so he wouldn't think his mother had abandoned him. They felt a relationship between the two of them, in the absence of Megan, would be healthy. Kate wasn't so sure, but felt pressured just the same

"Everyone makes mistakes, right Joe?" She asked her husband one night while in bed.

"They do," he answered without much thought.

"Don't they deserve the chance to prove they are sorry and try to redeem trust again from those they hurt?"

"Where are you going with this, Kate?"

"I've been pondering the possibility of a reunion with Andrew," she admitted.

Joe sat up and turned on the light. "I understand he's your son, and I've seen how hard this has been on you. Do you think you can overlook what he has done, though?"

"I think I'm willing to do my part by putting it behind us and giving him a second chance. I'll never forget the horrible things he did to his sister. Ever. They will be burned in my mind until the day I die."

Joe took his wife's hand within his. "You know I'll support you in whatever you feel you must do. I can watch Megan on my days off while you visit with him."

"Thank you. Right now, I'm not sure if I can go through with it, but someday I may want to."

"Take your time and listen to your heart," he urged, turning off the light. "Don't do it just because everyone wants you to."

Two months after Andrew abused his sister, Kate gained enough courage to speak with him for the first time. Sweat dripped from the back of her neck as she dialed Ed's house phone. *It'll be okay. We'll keep everything casual, with no pressure on either of us. It's just a mother reconnecting with her son.*

"Hello."

"Andrew, it's me, Mom." Kate tried to sound upbeat.

"Umm...hi," he said with a hint of caution in his voice.

"I thought it might be nice to go to the mall today. Would you like to come?

The long hesitation before he answered was enough to make her want to hang up. "Why?" he quipped.

She could almost hear his eyes rolling as he spoke, which didn't make it any easier on her to try and recreate a bond with him. "Because I haven't seen you in a while," she said flatly.

Andrew remembered the last time his mother had picked him up- she had brought him to the police station. He wanted to be sure he wasn't getting tricked again. "Who else will be there?"

"No one. Just you and me, I promise. We'll go to the mall and then right back home. What do you think?"

Andrew looked at the empty house around him. His father had been gone for hours, and he had no idea when he would be back, if at all that night. The kitchen cupboards were bare, and he knew if he went with his mother she would treat him to a nice meal. "Umm...sure, I guess so."

"Good. I'll be right there to get you."

Kate left Megan with Jo and made the old familiar trip to her ex-husband's. Each turn of the road brought her right back to the last time she had driven in that direction-- and all the events that had come with it. She shook the memories off every few minutes and cranked up the radio to drown them out.

She pulled into the shambled driveway in front of Ed's home and honked the horn. Andrew peeked out the window and made his way toward the vehicle. As he got in, Kate inched over to gain more space between them. The conversation stopped at hello, making the awkwardness between them very apparent.

Her palms were so sweaty they kept sliding off the wheel. Gripping it tighter, Kate fixed her eyes toward the road as Andrew turned up the radio. They let the music fill the silence between them.

Millions of questions burned inside of her, and by the time they reached the shopping center she couldn't wait a minute longer for the answers she so desperately needed. Kate found a parking space at the farthest end of the mall parking lot and turned the car off. Slowly, she turned to look at him.

"Why did you do it?" she asked in a calm voice.

Andrew shrugged his shoulders and looked away.

"Where would you have learned to do such a thing?" she urged.

This time he looked down at the floor. "I didn't want to do it, but he made me." Andrew's voice was quiet and trembling.

Kate's heart skipped a beat. "Who made you...what did they make you do?" she demanded. "Did somebody do something to you? What happened?"

"Nothing," he yelled. "This isn't what I came here for, and I'm not going to talk about it."

His reaction scared Kate. *Was he telling me he had been abused himself? Was that how he learned to do such things? Who could he have been talking about?* Her first instinct was to call the police. She wanted Andrew to disclose his trauma to them. He needed justice for the pain in his life. She needed to know what had happened to him.

Instead, chose to sit quietly. Deep down, she knew Andrew would recant his story before the police got there, and any chance she had of reconnecting with him would be lost. Not knowing what else to do, she slowly opened the car door to go inside to shop.

After a couple of purchases and a quick lunch, the feeling of overextending the welcome came over the two. Anxious to drop Andrew off, Kate drove as fast as she could back to his place. They tossed out casual goodbyes as if the whole encounter had been normal, and Kate drove away without even watching him walk into the house safely.

She took the scenic route home while allowing her emotions to get the best of her. *Had I unknowingly put him in a situation where he had been taken advantage of?* Her brain tried to recall every possible scenario the past years had brought; summer camp, a friend's house, possibly a family member? She couldn't place anything or anyone in particular, but had a vivid memory of how abusive Ed had been toward her, which weighed heavily on her mind. Could the abuse have been different for the kids? The thought of the children's father using them for sexual purposes disgusted her, yet she couldn't shake the feeling it could be a possibility.

CHAPTER TWELVE

May 2001

Kate managed to keep her visits with Andrew just long enough to prove to him he still had a mother. Keeping his promise to his wife, Joe stayed with Megan, being kind enough to cover up any questions pertaining to her mother's whereabouts she asked him each time. It made Kate feel like a traitor.

Trying to keep her daughter from knowing she spent time with the person who violated her was hard enough, but trying to physically keep her away from the people the judge ordered her to be around was much more difficult. Kate lied through her teeth every weekend Ed was supposed to have Megan, saying she was sick, busy, or at a sleepover. It kept Megan safe, but cost Kate another court appearance when Ed turned her in for not abiding by the judge's orders.

"Good luck today," Joe told his wife before heading out the door to work that morning. "I wish I could be there with you. I hate the thought of you doing this on your own."

"I think I'll be okay. I'm confident the judge will have no problem understanding why I haven't been letting Megan visit with Ed. I only have her best interest at heart by trying to protect her."

Joe pulled his wife in for a long hug. "I agree. We're only doing what's best for Megan. The judge has to realize that."

Resting her head on her husband shoulders, Kate sighed. "I'm sure he will."

***

"She isn't allowing Megan to visit with her father, which is strictly in violation of the last court order. Each time my client attempted to see his daughter, an excuse was made as to why she wasn't available," Ed's new lawyer, Mr. Zimmerman clamored.

"Is this true?" Judge Lagoe asked. Kate nodded slowly as the judge looked back at the lawyer.

"Mr. Preston isn't keeping her son away from her, and he deserves equal access to his daughter."

"Your honor," Kate defended herself, "My daughter is scared to go with her father and does not wish to go back there. What kind of mother would I be if I sent my child to a place where she didn't feel safe?"

"Your daughter is only nine-years-old and suffers from autism. She is not entitled to make her own decisions. Now, if you don't follow my ruling and allow her father to take her as ordered, you will spend time in jail for contempt. And once you are there, your ex-husband will gain temporary custody of your daughter. Do we understand each other?"

Kate didn't understand, but nodded to keep her freedom and gain time to figure out a plan to keep Megan out of danger.

"Good," he said. "This weekend you will take Andrew from five o'clock Saturday evening until four o'clock on Sunday evening. Mr. Preston will have Megan for visitation during the same time. Now make sure I don't see you back here for parental interference. We are adjourned."

The dirty grin on Ed's face when they walked out into the hallway turned Kate's stomach, but knowing she was battling a twisted justice system was what actually made her lose control. Kate was being forced to put her baby into harm's way by the very people who were supposed to be protecting her. By the time she reached her car in the parking lot, Kate nearly passed out from stress. Turning the keys, she drove straight to Karen's house. She wouldn't be home from work for another half-hour, but Kate would wait in the drive way until she arrived, and use that time to call Joe at work to give him an update on what happened in court.

***

"How am I going to tell Megan when she comes home from school today that she has to go back to visit with her father even though she is afraid of him? She'll think I don't care enough to protect her." Kate's hands trembled as she spoke and Karen gently placed hers over top to settle them.

"Is the judge really forcing you to send her there?"

"Yes. And things could get a lot worse for her if the judge finds out I violated the order. He threatened to put me in jail then said he would give Ed temporary custody of Megan."

"Then you have to do it, Kate. Just for now until we can figure out how to work around it. You know Joe and I would never want to put Megan at risk, but if you don't allow her to go there, the risk of Ed getting her is greater." While Kate knew Karen was thinking long term, she couldn't get past the idea of allowing her daughter to go, for even one second, with a man she feared.

The second Joe got home from work, Kate elaborated on what the judge was forcing her to do and how Andrew could be spending the weekend with them.

"I'm going to tell my boss I can't work the out of town job this weekend. I won't let you stay alone in the house with Andrew overnight," Joe insisted.

"If you can get the time off, that would be great. I'm a little uncomfortable with all of this," she admitted as Joe pulled her closer for a hug. "What would I do without you?"

"You're never going to have to find out."

***

As the Saturday approached, the gut wrenching decision to allow Megan to go with Ed consumed her. Kate waited until breakfast that morning to break the news. "Tonight your father is going to take you overnight," she casually blurted out as Megan was putting a spoonful of Cheerios into her mouth.

Megan didn't say a word but tears ran down her tiny young cheeks.

"Oh honey, it's going to be okay. I'm going to call you often to check on you and we'll pack your teddy bear to keep you company while you sleep."

Her brows knitted in a frown as she edged closer to her mother.

"You know I love you, but tonight is my turn to spend time with Andrew. You've got nothing to worry about because you'll be back home before you know it."

Megan sat quietly for a moment thinking, and only responded with "I love you, Mommy."

"I love you too, Puddin'. Now go get dressed. We've got time to go to the park before your father comes."

"Yeah, the park!" she exclaimed, as she scrambled up

to her room. It was all Kate could do not to run after her and hold her tight in her arms. She thought of driving to a park in a faraway state and never returning, but knew running away was not the answer.

When Ed pulled into the driveway at five o'clock, Kate gave Megan a big hug and kiss as she buckled her into the back seat of the car. Joe set her overnight bag in the seat next to her then made his way to the opened driver's side window. He stuck his head in and waved to his stepdaughter as her mother got her settled in. "Touch a hair on that little girl's head," he breathed to Ed, "and I'm coming after you."

Ed cocked his head in Joe's direction, narrowed his eyes and gave a radiating stare as he peeled out of the driveway the second Kate had shut the back door, without uttering a single word to his son. Kate watched them leave and prayed her little girl would be all right.

Joe put a reassuring hand on his wife's shoulder then picked up Andrew's bag and carried it into the house. Andrew followed inside the house and looked around.

"You'll be sleeping on the couch, so why don't you bring your things out to the living room," Kate suggested. It was the first time he'd been there since he was accused of rape, and she felt very uneasy having him around.

"Whatever," he fired back and tossed his duffle bag on the sofa.

She knew this was uncomfortable for all of them, and tried her best to ease the situation. "What do you want to do tonight?" she asked.

"I don't want to do anything," he grunted as he plopped himself down in front of the television. Not wanting to tread on rifting waters, she walked out of the room to find her husband.

"I can't just stand here and pretend everything is

normal," Kate vented. "Watching him sit around with a vague less expression is giving me the creeps. See if you can get him to agree to go do something."

Joe peered out at his stepson, who was transfixed on a TV show. "That's a good idea. I think if we let him sit there alone for too long, it will be much harder for him to reconnect with us. Let me go see what I can do," he offered.

Joe walked out to the living room and sat on the arm of the couch closest to Andrew. "What are you watching?"

His eyes rolled over in the direction of his stepfathers' and met his straight on. "A movie," he quipped.

Joe picked up the remote, turned the volume up a few notches, and pretended to feign interested in the show. "Is it any good?"

Andrew sighed at Joe's lame attempt to connect with him. "I guess," he muttered.

The two sat in awkward silence for a moment before Joe handed Andrew the remote. He drummed his fingers along his leg, trying to think of something to say that may peak Andrew's attention. "Your mom is making your favorite chicken cordon bleu for dinner tonight. How about before she starts it I treat us all to ice cream," he suggested.

"Fine," he reluctantly said getting on his shoes.

It was a warm day down by the river. Now that spring was upon them they could watch the boats sail by as the fishermen baited their hooks off the side of the vessel. Joe and Kate enjoyed the scenic view, holding hands as they walked, but Andrew seemed distracted. "Can we go? My butt hurts from walking."

Joe flashed his wife a disconcerting look. Kate shrugged her shoulders and threw up her hands, unsure of what his comment had meant. "What do you mean your butt hurts?" she questioned Andrew.

"Just what I said. It hurts. Can we go home now?"

A red flag immediately flashed into her head, but she knew if she pressed the issue right then things would turn ugly.

"Don't you want ice cream?" Joe asked.

Andrew shook his head. "Not really. I just want to back to the house."

"Okay, let's go," Kate decided. "It will be getting dark soon, anyways."

As soon as they returned home, Kate phoned Megan to check on her before she fell asleep. She couldn't wait to have her little girl back in her arms, where she would be safe. Concerns filled her head whether or not she should send Andrew back with Ed. Was he safe?

On Sunday morning, Kate woke up early and cooked Andrew his favorite rainbow-sprinkled pancakes for breakfast. She knew that at his father's house he wasn't fed decent meals so it felt good providing for him.

After breakfast, Kate suggested they go for another walk. Andrew refused again, still complaining it hurt too much whenever he walked. She couldn't think of any reason he would be having such a problem in his bottom area except if somebody had hurt him, and made up her mind to call the doctor on Monday morning to have him seen.

At four o'clock that evening, she drove to Ed's house so they could switch the kids back. Andrew didn't want to go back with his father, and strangely enough, when she picked up Megan she seemed hesitant to come home, even though she had phoned four times for Kate to come get her within the past twenty-four hours. She finally persuaded her to get in the car by promising her a ride in the front seat, a luxury not too often allowed because she was still under the age of twelve. The bribe worked, and as they headed for home, she filled her mother in on the details of what she did at her father's house. Megan kept hugging her mom and telling her how much she loved her the whole ride back.

After they ate dinner, Kate filled up a bubble bath for Megan before bed. The sound of her splashing and playing with her toys echoed out into the hallway, and then she heard her call her name. Kate peeked in to see what she wanted.

"Mom, can you look at my butt?" she asked as she pushed her torso out for to see. "It hurts."

Kate was frozen in time. She had just heard the same words from Andrew, and now her daughter comes home from her father's house saying it too. "What happened to it?"

"When my real dad was giving me a bath he put the soap inside me and it hurt."

Kate stared at her for a few moments, trying to comprehend what she had said. "Did he wash you on the outside with the soap, or on the inside?"

"On the inside, in my front butt and back butt." Her almond shaped eyes sloped down at the corners as she spoke.

Kate knelt down and took her daughter's face in her hands. "Honey, did he do to you what your brother did?"

Megan simply nodded, and buried herself in her mother's arms.

"Puddin', what did you do when he did that to you?"

Dropping her gaze, Megan clung tighter to her mother. "I was scared. It hurt and I told him to stop and he did."

Kate was crushed. How could this little girl go through such incredible cruelty twice within three months by two different people? "Let's go dry off," she suggested as she handed Megan a towel. "You get dressed and I'll go pop a movie in for you."

"Okay, Mama."

Slipping out of the bathroom door, Kate closed it behind her in a quiet rush. Her hands flew over mouth, aghast at what she just heard.

"What's wrong?" Joe asked, seeing his wife in distress.

"He did it to her, too," she managed between huffed breaths. "My bastard of an ex-husband hurt his own daughter last night."

"What?" Joe exploded. "That piece of shit better hope he dies a fiery death before I get to him."

"I can't deal with this right now," Kate cried tossing her hand up in the air. "What do we do?"

Looking at his wife who was so worn and desperate, Joe centered himself and focused on the women in his life who needed them. He needed to be logical for their sake. "Let's face it," he admitted. "Sitting in the emergency room again for hours upon hours isn't going to make a bit of difference. We've been down that road before and it got us nowhere, expect Megan subjected to a horrible exam."

"I can't make her go through that again," Kate gulped.

"No, defiantly not. It's pretty late right now anyways. Let's use this evening to set our emotions aside, and deal with it tomorrow morning when we have a more rational head on us."

"Alright," she agreed. "But I'm going to sleep on the floor in Megan's room tonight. I don't want her out of my sight."

"Agreed. Since I took this weekend off, there's no way I can call in sick for tomorrow, but we're going to figure out how to handle this."

Before leaving for work the next morning, Joe suggested to his wife that she call Megan's pediatrician for an appointment, then let her guide them as to what steps they should take next. Kate agreed it would be a good place to start and dialed the number as Joe kissed her goodbye.

The doctor's office was able to get them in immediately. When they arrived, they bypassed the waiting room, and were escorted directly back to a private area. The doctor followed them in with a handful of stickers for Megan to choose from.

"Good morning, sweetie," said Doctor Sanders. "Did you know that part of my job is to work with children who have been hurt and try to help them?"

Megan took one of the stickers from her and started peeling off the back to stick in on her shirt.

"Can you tell me what happened to you?"

"My butt hurts," Megan replied while taking the sticker back off and moving it to a new spot.

Doctor Sanders sat on the exam table next to Megan and put her arms around her. "How come it hurts, honey?"

"My father put the soap inside of me when he was washing me. I don't like that," Megan uttered between the tears that had started to fall.

The doctor darted her eyes to Kate, then back to her patients'. "Has your father done that to you before?" she asked.

Megan hesitated. A scowl crept up on her face and she stared up at the ceiling before answering. "Yes," she muttered as she started counting the tiles above her.

Dr. Sanders tried to refocus her by placing a hand on her cheek and turning her face towards her. "When?"

Moving her eyes from the ceiling to the pictures on

the wall, Megan slowly began rocking back and forth. "At his house."

"Was anybody else at his house when this happened?"

Megan fiddled with the corner of the paper sheet on the exam table until it ripped. "No."

"Did he touch you anywhere else?"

"He touched me all over," Megan confessed. "I don't like that." She started counting the ceiling tiles again from where she left off.

"I'm sorry, sweetie. Why don't you sit tight for a minute while your mommy and I step outside?"

"Okay," Megan said.

Kate handed her daughter a book from the bin on the floor and followed the doctor out of the room. Closing the door, the doctor and Kate huddled in the hall and talked in hushed voices. "Andrew was complaining his bottom was hurting all Saturday night. He wouldn't tell me why it hurt, but he kept saying it over and over. I'm really concerned."

"I'm going to place a hotline call to Child Protective Services. I'll pass along what Megan disclosed today."

"What do I do in the meantime?"

"Keep her close to you and let her know you love her. If you need anything else, don't hesitate to call."

Taking a deep breath, Kate opened the exam room door and told Megan they were ready to leave.

A callback from CPS arrived by dinnertime and Kate was asked if she could come directly to their office the following day to give a statement. She agreed to make the twenty-minute drive there, hoping this time they would take her daughter's word more seriously.

Neither her or Megan slept well that night, and were both up before Joe got ready for work the next morning. After they said their goodbyes, Kate and Megan got in the car, not mentally ready to endure another round of questioning.

For two and a half hours, Megan was asked questions no child should ever have to answer. Because of her disability, some of them were beyond her comprehension. Kate sat beside her and watched as she struggled to understand what they were asking. She was forced to ask, yet again, if they could explain things in simpler terms for her. The woman conducting the interview finally agreed and tried a different approach.

She found an anatomically correct drawing of a woman standing naked, facing both forward and backwards, and asked Megan to name all the parts of the body.

"Is that really necessary?" Kate asked. "She's just a little girl."

"I know it isn't easy, but one of the warning signs of sexual abuse in young children is if they use adult words to label their body parts instead of using age appropriate language. We need to see what your daughter has been exposed to."

The case worker pointed to each part of the body and wrote down next to it the word Megan used to name it. Then Megan was asked to point on the picture where her father had touched her. She remained consistent with saying he had touched her in the "front butt and back butt," pointing to the corresponding areas on the paper.

"You did a great job, Megan. All the parts are now labeled. If you want, you can go in the room over there to play with toys while your mom and I talk."

Megan looked at her mother, who flashed a smile to let her know it would be okay. She watched her walk out into the hallway, then Kate braced herself for what was coming.

"I know this is hard for you, but without more evidence, the act itself could be considered normal bathing. Even though she disclosed the same information she told the doctor, unless she is able to give more detailed information, it is going to be her word against her father's."

Kate was dumbfounded. What kind of justice system were they living in? Her daughter was victimized twice and because she was disabled, they were not going to take her word for it.

"Isn't there anything you can do?" Kate pleaded.

"We could talk with her brother and see if he could corroborate her story. If he tells us he's seen his father doing something to her, or if he is being abused himself, then we could take the information more seriously. Would you like to bring him in so we could talk with him?"

"No," Kate snapped. She learned her lesson the first time. All she'd heard from everyone was what a bad mother she was for bringing her own child down to the police station. Nobody mentioned they were proud of her for doing whatever it took to protect her other child. No, she would not be putting herself in the same situation again.

"Andrew won't come willingly to talk about it. Can somebody place a visit to his house, or at school to interview him?"

"I'm sorry, but that's not possible. The only way for us to talk with him is if you bring him to us."

Once again, all of the responsibility lay on Kate's shoulders. The justice system should be stepping up to protect its citizens. She walked away defeated, knowing she would be facing this battle alone. She vowed to keep Megan away from her father on her own, no matter what the consequences would be for her.

It was clear nobody was going to take Megan seriously, so Kate had to step up her game and figure out how to protect her daughter. Her first priority was to file another petition with the court and ask the judge if he would vacate the visitation order between Megan and Ed. With another hotline call in the records, she hoped it might weigh a little differently in the judge's eyes. Until they were in the courtroom, she would avoid Ed at all cost. Three weeks later, they found themselves being sworn in once again for testimony.

"Your court files are getting fat awfully quick. Why did you find it necessary to submit more paperwork?" Judge Lagoe asked Kate.

"My daughter's pediatrician had to place a hotline call against Ed. Megan disclosed to her that her father abused her during their last visitation together. I would like you to consider revoking his visitation rights with my daughter."

"That bitch is making up lies about me," Ed yelled from his table.

"This is a court of law and curse words will not be allowed, Mr. Preston. Do you understand?"

"My client apologizes, your honor," Mr. Zimmerman interjected.

"Very well," responded the judge. "Now since there was no witness to verify Megan's statements, her testimony could not be accepted without more details from her. Your request is denied."

"Your honor, please," Kate begged. "My daughter is terrified of going to her father's house."

"My order stands."

Desperate, she attempted one last request. "Can you at least tell Mr. Preston he should not be washing Megan while she is with him?"

"Do you wash her?" Judge Lagoe asked in surprise.

"Yes," Ed retorted.

Flipping through the files for her demographic information, he couldn't find what he wanted quick enough. "How old is she?" he asked.

"Megan is nine," Ed told him.

"At nine-years-old she should be washing herself. Why are you doing it?"

"She begs me to bathe her. Plus, if I don't do it, she doesn't wash all of the bubbles off. Basically, I'm doing it for her health," Ed replied.

Kate's jaw dropped at his statement. It was the most disgusting thing she had ever heard. Did Ed really think the judge would believe she begs him to wash her?

"She's old enough to wash herself, so you need to stop doing it for her. The restraining order petition that has been filed is hereby deemed unnecessary and is therefore dismissed. The current visitation schedule stands valid," the judge ruled.

In desperation, Kate attempted one last plea. "Your honor, I feel it is a conflict of interest for the children to share a law guardian since Andrew's trial is still pending. I would like to request they each have separate representation."

"Very well," he noted. "Andrew will now be represented by Mr. Fred Dillon, and Megan will be represented by Mrs. Chelsea Miller. They will be contacting you shortly to set up an initial meeting. We will reconvene at a later date to hear the results of Andrew's sexual offender assessment. Until then, court is adjourned."

Another defeat, but this time Kate at least had a small victory to celebrate. The law guardian assigned to Megan was very nice and easy to talk to. She understood the delicate manner of Megan's disability and worked well around it. Wanting to get the most accurate information out of their time together, she decided to schedule several different meetings with Megan to be held at different locations. Initially, she would meet Megan, Kate, and Joe together at their home. The next time, she wanted to meet Megan alone at her school. Kate knew this was because she wanted to see if Megan had a different story when her parents weren't around. Kate was more than happy to let her see for herself how Megan never veered from her statements.

After they met for the last time, Chelsea called Kate to discuss her opinions on the case and what she felt was necessary to protect Megan.

"Megan openly talked about the things her brother and father have done to her. She's stated several times she is scared of them. I believe your daughter is telling the truth."

"You don't know how good it is to hear those words. So many people have dismissed her because of her disability. I just want to keep her safe."

"Don't worry. I'm going to write a summary of my findings and recommend to the court all visitations be suspended."

A sense of relief started to overcome Kate, as this was the first time things looked like they might go in their favor in court.

CHAPTER THIRTEEN

Kate finally came to terms with having to cover the cost for Andrew's therapy. It was an unfair paradox to have to pay for her daughter's abuser, though she wanted Andrew to get the help he needed. As a mother, she couldn't deny that. Still, Kate couldn't help but feel as if her position was somehow being exploited.

With the $100 co-pay in hand, she drove to a place called Second Chances Therapeutic Services. The irony of the company's name seemed absurd; second chances for sexual offenders? She wasn't ready to accept they had that right.

Kate parked the car behind the building and slowly made her way into the office. Her hands twitched slightly as she handed the money to the receptionist. In return, she handed Kate a large packet to fill out on Andrew's past behaviors. The questionnaire wanted to know about sexual history, disciplinary practices used at home, and how the parents dealt with these issues. Q. 9: *If your child is a male, does he use the bathroom sitting down? Q.23: Does he insist on dressing in girl clothes or wearing make up? Q.33: Is your child afraid of being around people of the opposite sex? Q. 46: Has your child ever urinated or defecated in places other than the toilet?*

Kate could only assume the questions were aimed at

trying to find out if somebody had been abused, and if so, if it was by a male or female offender. She answered every question as honestly as possible then handed it back to the receptionist.

"Has Andrew's father made his first appointment with the therapist yet?" Kate asked, praying Ed would be responsible enough to make sure it was done on time.

"We have not heard from him at all," she told her, shaking her head. Kate rolled her eyes in disgust as she handed over the forms.

The receptionist took the paperwork and glanced them over to make sure Kate had answered every one of the questions. "Jolene Hilton, the therapist you'll be seeing, will be contacting you prior to finalizing her evaluation for the court."

Kate was starting to become impatient. "All I need to know is if the evaluation will be done in time for the next court appointment."

"Hold on for a moment," she said, and walked to the back room. Moments later she returned with a large lady who followed behind her. Her dark hair was short and spiky, and her voice as gruff as her looks. "Hello, I'm Jolene," she introduced herself. I'll be doing your son's evaluation."

"Nice to meet you," Kate replied.

"It would really help Andrew's assessment if you could bring Megan here so I could meet her."

Kate's eyebrows shot up. *Bring my daughter to meet the therapist who was evaluating her offender? Is this woman out of her mind?* She had to think carefully before responding. "I don't feel it's appropriate to bring a child who has been sexually abused to a place where sexual offenders would be sitting in the waiting room. It's a little creepy to me. Like fresh meat sitting in an open field where coyotes roam. Why would meeting the victim help the perpetrator anyway?"

"It's an important part of the process. How about if I make the appointment for a time when no one else would be here? Will that be easier for you?" she persisted.

Once again, Kate let her sense of responsibility override her better judgment. "I guess it would be okay."

"Good. How about you come tomorrow afternoon at two o'clock?"

"Sure," Kate relented, feeling bullied into it. Jolene smiled and Kate nearly tripped over a chair as she tried to get out of the office as fast as she could.

***

Kate hated walking into the place. Knowing it was a breeding ground for people with sexual addictions sent chills down her spine. She felt dirty just being there, and disgusted for having her daughter with her as well. They opened the door to the small office and Kate made both of them stand while they waited to see the therapist, in an effort to avoid sitting in a place where criminals had been. It was easier to walk around and talk to Megan about the pictures on the wall than explain to her daughter why she didn't want her to sit in a chair.

"Kate, so nice to see you again. Why don't you and Megan come on back into my office?" Jolene's voice seemed even deeper than last time.

Taking Megan's hand, Kate slowly followed Jolene into the office and huddled with her daughter on the couch that sat directly in front of Jolene's chair.

"Now, Megan," Jolene started, wasting no time. "Tell me about your brother, Andrew."

Megan's eyes shriveled down toward her nose. She gripped on to her mother's arm as she spoke. "I'm mad at him. I don't want to see him anymore!"

Jolene made several notes on the paper in front of her, then tapped the pen against her chin. She wasn't sure what to make of this little girl's attitude. "I see. How come?"

"Because he's mean to me!" Megan answered in a voice just short of a scream. Kate tried to comfort her daughter so she would calm down.

Jolene leaned back in her chair, studying the dynamics between mother and daughter. "Can you tell me how he is mean to you?"

"He's mean," she repeated.

"Megan, if you can tell me how your brother is being mean to you, then I can work with him on trying to be nicer."

Megan pivoted her body away from Jolene. "I don't want him to come over any more," she told her mother.

Kate nodded her head. "I know."

"I have some coloring books out in the other room," Jolene directed Megan. "Why don't you color me a picture while I talk to your mom?"

Megan glanced up at her mom to see if it was okay. Kate waved her on so she and Jolene could talk.

"Kate, I think in this situation you are lucky your daughter has special needs."

"What are you talking about?" Kate asked defensively. Her dislike for this woman was growing by the minute.

"It doesn't appear she remembers anything Andrew did to her. Consider yourself blessed she's not haunted by it."

Kate was mortified! "My daughter does remember what happened to her. She remembers everything and it affects her life every day. Megan has nightmares, wets the bed, and is plagued by flashbacks. She constantly makes comments about her father and brother being mean to her and how she doesn't want to see them anymore. How dare you tell me I'm lucky?"

"Kate, I think you're making too much of it. Clearly it has left her mind and she has gotten on with her life. Children like her don't let stuff bother them."

Trying to hold back from ripping her apart, Kate picked up her purse and walked out to get Megan. "If you need to talk more I will have to come back when Megan is not with me. I wouldn't want to overreact in front of her."

"I'll have my receptionist call and set up a time two weeks from now. That will give me an opportunity to meet with Andrew one-on-one, and see him in a group setting once or twice."

Kate seethed as they walked down the steps to the car. What nerve of her to think people with disabilities didn't remember things, when the truth is they remember every detail but they choose to forgive instead. Most people with disabilities believe everybody wants to be their friend and since they don't have a lot of close relationships, they are willing to overlook any shortcomings to keep that friendship. Even typical children who are being abused don't wish to have harm come to their perpetrator; they just want the abuse to stop. It doesn't mean they forgot what they have been through. This person was supposed to be a professional, and she was shocked Jolene didn't know this.

As much as Kate wanted to debate Jolene's theory, she dreaded going back to see her again. They were already going through a very vulnerable time, and didn't need somebody adding fuel to the fire by discrediting her daughter because of her disability.

As Kate walked up the flight of stairs to Jolene's office on their next scheduled appointment, she could feel the familiar turning in her stomach that reminded her of where she was about to enter. Kate took a deep breath and proceeded down the hallway, only to freeze in her steps when she realized she was not the only one in the waiting room this time. She quickly dropped her gaze to the floor so she wouldn't have to make eye contact with anyone, and then stood in the corner farthest away from the seating area. It seemed like forever until it was her turn to go in the therapy room. Kate was grateful when her name was called so she could escape the presence of the criminals sitting around her.

Jolene sat in her padded computer chair and started the session with a presumption that made Kate's heart skip at least three beats.

"After reviewing Andrew's history, it appears Megan had been his only female victim that we are aware of. It's possible Andrew could have been going through an identity crisis and decided to perpetrate upon his sister because she was 'safe.' He most likely needed to prove to himself he was not gay."

Kate was so floored she didn't even know how to start responding to her. Her mind flooded back to the past year and a half when Andrew had started using the term *gay* an awful lot. It was a word he used to describe T.J. on numerous occasions, and found ways to throw it into his everyday vocabulary. *Could it be true, was he trying to prove his sexuality by having sex with a female?* Even so, it didn't make sense to her that he would take advantage of his sibling to prove such a theory.

"That doesn't make sense. Why would he target his sister?"

"Andrew isn't exactly what others would consider 'cool'. He would have a hard time approaching a female to gain access to her, so he took whatever was readily available to him. Andrew knew Megan was not going to fight him off, so that made her a safe target."

They sat in silence for a few moments while Jolene's statement simmered in her brain. There was so much Kate wanted to say, yet she was rendered speechless. The beat of her heart was pounding through her chest so fast she was finding it hard to breathe.

"Andrew told me during our session how he has seen his father having relations with random girls on the couch. He also claims that quite often Ed sits at the computer naked while using the web cam."

"Did you report this to Child Protective Services?"

Jolene shook her head. "They wouldn't be able to prove if Andrew saw things or not, and Ed could always argue that Andrew walked out into the living room late at night when he should have been sleeping. If he didn't mean for Andrew to see him with a woman, then it isn't considered endangering the welfare of a child."

"Well, it certainly isn't acceptable behavior knowing your child who has been accused of sex crimes is in the other room."

"In Ed's defense, he kept a towel nearby to cover himself if Andrew did wander into the living room."

"Are you kidding me?" Kate yelled loud enough for people in the waiting room to hear.

"Kate, it is not illegal for a grownup to have sex. As long as Ed made an attempt to keep himself unexposed there is nothing the law can do about it."

Huge red flags on Jolene's philosophies flashed through her mind.

"How has Andrew been during group therapy?" Kate asked trying to steer the conversation somewhere else.

Jolene scooped up a handful of m&m's from the dish on her desk and popped them in her mouth. She took her time savoring each bite before she answered Kate's question. "He's participating well and is conscious of his past actions. Actually, Ed finally finished his questionnaire. He minimized any past behavioral problems and stated all of Andrew's issues were due to a conflict between the two of you."

"That's not surprising," Kate retorted.

Holding out the dish to offer Kate a snack, she took another handful of chocolate and continued the conversation after Kate waved it away. "The judge is expecting my recommendation soon. I plan on telling him Andrew is at low risk of re-offending."

"And you came to this conclusion after only meeting him a few times in a group setting?"

The distinct roll of Jolene's eyes told Kate she was not used to having her authority challenged. "I'm also recommending for you to try to reconcile with your son and start establishing a cohesive relationship."

Kate pressed her lips together in a thin line. "Perhaps he should have thought about that before preying upon my daughter."

"He's just a child, Mrs. Rose. Kids make mistakes and it's up to the parents to show them love regardless."

Kate bent over and hung her head between her legs. Jolene steered the conversation in a whole new direction.

"What was your marriage like with Andrew's father?"

Kate's eyes widened as she straightened herself in the chair. "It was horrible. Ed is an angry, abusive person with severe control issues."

"And how was the sex?"

"Excuse me?" she shouted, her cheeks blushed with embarrassment.

"Mrs. Rose, I have reason to believe that throughout your marriage, Ed was trying to groom you."

Kate's stomach knotted. "Well, I certainly didn't enjoy having to do my martial duties with him. The thought of it sickened me, to say the least." Her mind raced at the suggested implications about her ex-husband.

"There may be some connection between Ed's sexual appetite and your son's indiscretions."

Looking back, Kate knew something wasn't quite right in their marriage. She always crunched the blankets between them at night so Ed wouldn't be able to touch her. Her personal space always felt violated. Suddenly, Kate felt extremely dirty. She was sickened at the thought of Ed spending years manipulating her mind so he could live in a demented world. Kate left Second Chances, drove straight home and ran towards the shower. She tried to scrub ten years of memories out of her mind.

CHAPTER FOURTEEN

There is no fury worse than that of a bitter ex-husband. Not allowing Megan to visit with her father had added fuel to the fire Ed had raged against Kate ever since she left him. Ed had an innate need to control everyone, especially his ex-wife, despite their divorce papers and her newly acquired marriage certificate to Joe. Kate knew he didn't really want to see his daughter. What he truly enjoyed was seeing his ex-wife in pain, and if it meant going after Megan, he was going to do it.

Joe and Kate were playing outside with Megan one evening when a patrol car pulled into the driveway. Ed's car pulled in directly behind it. There was no doubt in Kate's mind it was because she had not allowed Megan to go with him. Immediately, she rushed her daughter inside the house and told her to lock the door and close all the curtains. As usual, Megan did what she was told without asking any questions. Joe curled his arm around his wife's waist and tugged her closer to him as the trespassers got out of their cars and walked toward them.

"I want my daughter now!" screamed Ed as he raced toward Kate with the all-too-familiar look of hatred burning in his eyes.

"You can't have her," she yelled back at him.

Ed barged closer until he was inches from his ex-wife's face and brandished his fist. "If you don't hand her over now I'm going to have you arrested. The judge ordered I be allowed to take her on the weekends. If she isn't out here in five seconds I'm going in to get her myself."

Joe slid Kate behind him and stepped closer to Ed. "Do not threaten my wife," he warned.

"Everybody calm down," the police officer instructed. "Ma'am, do you have any paperwork stating what the custody schedule is?"

"Yes. I'll go grab it," Kate replied, grateful for the escape.

Megan opened the door for her mother and Kate frantically began to rifle through the stacks of letters she had received from the courts.

"What's going on, Mommy?" Megan asked watching the commotion from inside the house.

"I need to get some paperwork, honey; nothing for you to worry about."

Kate could hear Joe and Ed screaming at each other outside as she scrambled to find the paperwork. When she had the latest copy of their visitation schedule in hand, she told Megan to turn on some music and go upstairs to play. She wanted to drown out the skirmishing sounds coming in from the window. By the time Kate returned outside, things were getting heated.

"Sir, if you can't control yourself you will have to sit in the back of my car," threatened the cop.

Kate couldn't help snicker as she heard the cop put Ed in his place. She handed over the paperwork and hovered closer to her husband. "Here's the most recent copy of the judge's ruling. All it states is that Ed has rights to visitations every other weekend. He has not had Megan because she's afraid to go with him. There is an ongoing sexual abuse investigation in progress."

The cop briefly looked over the paperwork. Luckily, it had not been permanently modified from the court since they were still awaiting the outcome of the criminal case, so it was very vague. The simplicity of the wording was all the officer needed. "Sir, this does not state specifically this is your weekend. I cannot arrest her for parental interference. You're going to have to leave her residence."

"Not without my daughter," Ed demanded.

The cop was firm in his tone. "For the last time, Sir, you will need to leave."

Ed stared at him for a moment, then walked toward his car without a word. The officer started his own car and pulled out of the driveway. As soon as he was out of sight, Ed opened his door and bolted toward the house to get Megan. Kate raced him to the door to get to her first. Behind her, she could hear Joe and Ed arguing as she made it safely inside the house and watched from the window. Not knowing what else to do, her plan was to wait him out.

Joe spoke calmly, in an effort to get Ed to leave. "Why don't you let Kate call you tonight to work out a visitation schedule? Right now she's too emotional to talk."

Ed got within a hair's breadth from Joe's face and screamed. "My daughter is coming with me now!" Then without warning, he yanked Joe's shirt to pull him in closer and slammed him to the ground. The two rolled around in the dirt, each vying for the place on top.

Frantically, Kate called 911. She was told unless a weapon was involved, domestic situations were dealt with when there was an officer available. She begged the dispatcher to hurry, then her attention riveted to the window.

Ed's hands tightened around Joe's neck as he gasped for air. The commotion was so loud the neighbor ran over to help. Giving up waiting for the authorities, Kate threw the phone down and ran outside to assist her husband. By the time she got to his side, Joe was lying on the ground while their neighbor was trying to pry Ed off the top of him. Having the body mass equivalent to a sumo wrestler, Ed defiantly had the upper hand.

The neighbor managed to dislodge Ed enough for Joe to roll away, his neck covered with handprints. As soon as Joe was back on his feet, the two started to rumble again. Kate's pleas went unheard as they swung at each other, boxing it out in her front yard. Once the sirens were heard coming down the road, the two finally stopped fighting.

Not happy he had to return, the policeman placed Ed in the back seat of the patrol car while statements were taken from everyone. Even though Joe had sustained visible injuries, the police advised him it was not in his best interest to file assault charges. He offered to press charges for trespassing instead. Joe said it wasn't worth his time, but Kate insisted on filing the papers. After years of enduring physical abuse by Ed, she wasn't about to let him get away with another thing if she could help it.

Ed was issued a ticket and was warned not to return. Kate asked the officer to drive back by the house in a little while to make sure he didn't return again. Joe and Kate walked back inside the house and took pictures of his battered face and neck in case they needed photographic proof for court later on. It was a lesson she learned the hard way during her violent ten-year stint with Ed. Nothing seemed to surprise her when it came to her ex-husband, but she knew one thing was for sure. She would not allow him to continue to make her live a life in fear.

CHAPTER FIFTEEN

The month-long wait until the next court appearance seemed to take forever. Kate's anxiety heightened as she counted down to the date. They anticipated Andrew would be sentenced, and she had mixed emotions on what she hoped was to come. Andrew's caseworker secured a bed for him at a rehabilitation facility fifty miles south of where they lived. If the judge went with the recommendations, Andrew would be sent to the facility straight from the courthouse.

Kate's feelings were being tugged from both sides. On one hand, she knew Andrew would greatly benefit from having intense support from professional people who could get to the root of his demons. On the other hand, he was still her child and the thought of him being sent there scared her. In the end, Kate knew she had to opt for tough love if she wanted Andrew to be successful in his rehabilitation.

On the day of the fact-finding hearing, Joe and Kate dropped Megan off at school then drove to the courthouse together, mentally prepared for the worst. When they arrived, Andrew was already in the hall talking with his law guardian. He was expected to enter the witness stand and testify to his actions and they were prepping him with last minute defense tactics. Even though Andrew was the one on trial, both Ed and Kate secured their own lawyers; the first time Kate had done so through all their legal affairs.

Megan's law guardian was also there, which added to the mixture of professionals who filled the waiting room. Family members were split between both sides of the courtroom, as dedication to each child was chosen. It was standing room only, and the atmosphere was very tense as the judge entered the courtroom.

"Please rise," the bailiff instructed.

"You may now be seated," stated the judge. "Today we will be reviewing the case of a twelve-year-old juvenile who is accused of sexual misconduct. I understand he has agreed to a plea deal."

"That is correct your honor," announced the defense attorney.

"Very well," continued the judge. "The court will need to hear the testimony from the defendant. Andrew, would you please take the stand?"

Kate's stomach knotted as she glanced over at her son. He walked sullenly toward the witness stand. His face remained expressionless as he placed his youthful hand on the Bible.

"Do you promise to tell the truth, the whole truth, and nothing but the truth, so help you God?"

"Yes," muttered Andrew.

"Please state your full name for the record."

"Andrew Jacob Preston."

The defense attorney rose and walked toward the witness stand. "How old are you Andrew?"

"Twelve."

"Quite a young age to be facing crimes of this nature," his lawyer stated. Andrew just stared at him. "Because you are still considered a youth, you have the opportunity today to tell the court what your involvement was in the alleged crime, and in return you could be granted a youthful offender status. Do you know what that means?"

"Yes," Andrew answered. "It means as long as I don't get into any more trouble until I turn eighteen, my case will be sealed. Then I no longer will have a criminal record."

"Correct. But in order for that to happen, the judge will need to hear a confession from you. Are you willing to provide one?"

"Yes," he mumbled.

"Very well. Can you tell the court the specific reasons why you are here today?"

Kate closed her eyes as the details of the abuse she had tried so hard to push out of her mind now filled her ears. Andrew divulged in vivid detail how he had abused both T.J. and Megan. Kate couldn't bring herself to look at him, so she found a spot on the wall and stared at it while tears streamed down her face. She briefly stole a glance in Ed's direction to see his reaction. Both he and his mother Maureen seemed oblivious to the vicious words Andrew revealed.

Lawyers from both sides took turns questioning Andrew and he answered so aloofly Kate wondered whether or not he even felt any remorse for his actions. He didn't seem bothered by the possibility of being sent to a juvenile delinquency center.

When the recounting ended, the judge released Andrew from the stand and then turned his attention toward Kate. "Is there anything you would like to say, Mrs. Rose, before I make my decision?"

Joe nudged his wife to stand and voice her opinion. Dr. Covington's voice kept replaying in her head. *"One day he is going to do something that will land him at the mercy of the court system. Only then will he get the intensive treatment he needs."* Kate knew this would be her only chance of getting Andrew the help he needed to reform his life. She dug deep down inside her heart and gathered up all the tough love she could muster before she spoke.

"I believe it is in Andrew's best interest to get away from his father. He needs to learn how people can react to their feelings in ways other than violence. A facility will give him treatment. By allowing him to remain with Ed, you will be sending him the message that he got away with the crime. What will stop him from doing it again?"

As she spoke, she could feel the heat of Ed's anger as he stared her down from across the courtroom. It was a look she'd seen many times before, and knew there was going to be hell to pay. This time she wouldn't back down. She would fight for what her child needed, even if it made her look like a bad mother.

"Mr. Preston, where do you think the best place for your son is?" Judge Lagoe asked.

Ed stood up and started walking toward Kate as he began screaming. "Unlike Andrew's mother here, I do not want to ship my son off somewhere so I don't have to be bothered with him anymore. It's obvious she doesn't care for her child at all." He hovered over Kate's seat and had to be redirected back to his own table. "I want Andrew with me. With his family who will oversee his care. That's the best place for a twelve-year-old child."

He put on a good show for the courtroom; appearing to be caring and doting on his only son, and worried about his welfare. But Kate knew her ex-husband all too well. She'd seen how Ed treated family, and it wasn't pretty. She hoped the judge wouldn't buy into his act.

"Thank you, Mr. Preston. I believe I have heard enough to make a determination in the case," declared the judge.

"Andrew, you are officially charged with one count of endangering the welfare of a child. All other charges against you are hereby dropped."

Andrew smirked at his father, who congratulated him with a high-five from under the table as the judge continued with his verdict.

"You are ordered to serve one year of probation. Officer April Monet will oversee your supervision. You are also mandated to attend sexual offender counseling until discharged by the provider and to undergo a mental health evaluation. As part of your probationary period, you will need to fulfill forty hours of community service and work closely with a preventive care caseworker. You are hereby remanded to the custody of your father."

Kate's head dropped down into her hands as she sobbed uncontrollably. They had all lost. Megan lost her childhood. Kate lost a son. Andrew lost his opportunity to rehabilitate his life. Precious commodities--stolen.

"Mr. Preston," the judge continued, "because Andrew will be under your supervision, you will be required to cooperate with any and all agencies involved in his care. Do we understand each other?"

"Yes, your honor." The smug look on Ed's face mirrored his offspring; two conniving individuals who had no regard for anyone else. They felt entitled and knew they had just beaten the system.

"The criminal case is now dismissed. We will continue with the custody matter at hand. I have received the initial sexual offender evaluation from Jolene. She feels Andrew is at low risk of re-offending so I am going to reinstate visitation between the two children as long as they are supervised by an adult."

Kate's heart raced at the thought of having Andrew around Megan again and couldn't take any chances. "Your honor, it would be unrealistic to think anybody could keep their eyes on a child every minute of the day. Anytime I use the restroom, take a bath, or sleep at night, the kids would technically be unsupervised. I don't want to put Megan at risk again. As we learned from the last time, it only takes a few moments for something to happen. I beg you to keep the current visitation the same. That way we could alternate having only one child at a time each weekend like we have been."

The judge seemed appalled at the request. "How do you expect the kids to be together then?"

"I don't expect them to be together. Andrew abused Megan and confessed to it. We all just heard the testimony," Kate replied.

The judge looked at her with a no-nonsense stare. "They are siblings and need to be around each other," he insisted. "Request denied. I am rescinding the temporary custody order and declare that all future visitations each child has with their parent are to coincide with both children at the same time. They will be together with Mrs. Rose starting this weekend, then the following weekend they will be with Mr. Preston."

"But your honor," Kate pressed.

"Case dismissed," declared the judge as the swung his gavel.

The room emptied one by one. Lawyers and caseworkers flowed out as if everything that had just happened was normal. Joe remained on the bench trying to console his wife as she curled up into a ball at the corner of her seat. Livid. Distraught. Confused. Scared. Infuriated. She was all of these at once.

Kate wondered why everyone insisted it was in Megan's best interest to be around the person who had not only sexually abused her, but another child as well?

Basically, they were telling her what happened was okay because it was incest, and not some random crime with a stranger. Kate knew Megan wasn't emotionally ready to face her brother again. How was she going to feel having this person forced back into her life, or worse, living back in her house? Would she be able to sleep comfortably at night knowing he was there? Kate wasn't even sure if she could.

CHAPTER SIXTEEN

July 2001

"Megan, I need to tell you something," Kate told her daughter as they fed the ducks day-old bread down at the river one afternoon. "From now on your brother will be coming over on the weekends like he used to."

"Why?" her small voice cracked as she spoke. Kate wanted to explain how the court was making them follow a visitation schedule and it was out of her control, but she needed Megan to fully comprehend what she was talking about. She had to say something to ease her mind, even if it wasn't completely true.

"Andrew's sorry for what he did to you and he would like to come and visit again."

Megan studied the ducks as they bobbed their heads underwater and tossed them more food. She grunted out a "Humph," and turned away from her mother.

Kate couldn't blame her for the callous response. She felt the same way. "Don't worry, I'll make sure you're safe, okay?"

"I don't want him to hurt me again," she sobbed.

"Neither do I. I don't want anybody to hurt you." Kate tried to sound confident in her response and prayed she would be able to keep her promise to her daughter.

If the judge was making her have the kids together all weekend long, she would have to do something different with the sleeping arrangements. No longer did she trust him to sleep on the second level with Megan. He needed to be downstairs where she could keep her ears and eyes on hyper-alert at all times. The only solution she could come up with was to close off the double living room and convert part of it into a new bedroom. Joe would easily be able to accomplish it. All he would need was drywall, nails, and a can of paint to make it work. Andrew would have to continue sleeping on the couch until it was done.

Since they were redoing the room, she decided to get new bedding to go along with the décor. Fresh sheets and pillowcases gave the room a whole new look, and the feel of a fresh start. They brought the boxes of Andrew's belongings in from the garage where they had been stored for the past few months, and worked feverishly to complete the room. She concentrated all her efforts on finishing the project, wanting every detail to look its best. Several weeks later, Kate was eager to show Andrew his new sleeping quarters, though her excitement was short lived.

"Why can't I have a bedroom door with a lock on it?" he asked snidely looking at the room with disgust.

Kate's hopes for a new start were crushed. She knew what he really meant. There was no way that was going to happen. He was lucky he had a door at all.

Every creak the house made jolted her awake each time he stayed over. She tossed and turned all night, constantly getting up to go to the bathroom as an excuse to check on both the kids. By daybreak, she was exhausted. As nervous as she was about Megan, her daughter seemed quite resilient having Andrew back in the house. She stayed quiet and mostly kept to herself, but there were no tears or nightmares. Kate took it as a good sign of the progress Ann made with her in her recovery.

For Kate, it was hard mentally having everyone together again. She felt that one can never really put the past behind them without it creeping up every once in a while reminding them why their life had changed in the first place. She tried to remain optimistic though, hoping this could be the start of a new beginning for them. As the weeks progressed, she felt certain her family would overcome their past.

CHAPTER SEVENTEEN

April was the glue that kept each of the agencies involved, connected, and informed. She facilitated all communications between interested parties and worked hard to ensure everyone was on the same page before dealing with either Andrew or Ed. It wasn't always easy coordinating things between everyone involved in Andrew's care, but she somehow managed to make it work.

"You know," April sighed during one of her visits with Kate, "Andrew still has to complete his forty-hours of community service in order to satisfy his probationary agreement."

"I know," Kate sighed. "I've actually been waiting to see if Ed will step up to the plate and start taking some responsibility for something. All he would have to do is drop his son off and pick him back up when he was done. For once, I would like to see him be the one inconvenienced."

"Kate, I know you've done a lot to facilitate all the help Andrew needs, but I would hate to see him be penalized for not completing his probationary terms because Ed won't allow him to do any service. I know a few places around town here accepting kids like him."

"Please understand my side. Twice a week I drive forty minutes to pick up Andrew at Ed's house, drive another hour to get him to therapy, then bring him back to his father's house afterwards. I don't mind doing it. After all, it is an effort to help my child, but it does get tiring after a while. His father should share in the responsibility. Ed needs to take a small part in all of this. Let him be the one to ensure Andrew finishes his community service requirements."

"I agree with your rational. I'm hesitant to believe Ed will actually follow through with it, but I'm willing to try to force it upon him. Because Ed's name was signed under the probation terms along with Andrew's, he is still legally accountable."

"Thanks for understanding, April," Kate smiled.

By the end of the school year, Ed still had not taken the initiative to find Andrew a place where he could start his community service. April once again asked Kate if she would find a place for him to work so he didn't breach his contract. Within a week, Kate had him signed up to do light cleaning duties at a local recreation center. She worked out the schedule for Andrew to work a two hour shift on the Saturday when she had him for visitation. Until his forty-hours were completed, Kate was committed to using her time with Andrew to force him to work. Once again, she was the bad guy in his eyes.

Andrew resisted going on the first day. It took a threat of calling April to get him in the car. He sat stiff, his arms folded tight against his chest. Kate ignored the fact that he was pouting and drove in silence to the recreation center. After she introduced him to his new supervisor, she took Megan for a walk to the playground while they waited for his time to be up. Part of her was glad he was being forced to work; she hoped the responsibility would mature him a little. Kate wanted nothing more than to see him develop into a dependable teenager. She half-expected Andrew to be totally miserable when she arrived at the end of his shift, but to her surprise, found him playing pool with another kid instead.

"Hi," Andrew boasted as shot the eight ball into the corner pocket and cleared the table.

The supervisor looked up from the newspaper he was reading, saw Kate was there to pick up Andrew, and walked toward them as he signed off on Andrew's attendance sheet "He did a great job. We'll see him next week."

Kate was a little taken aback with the aloof atmosphere. "See you then," she nodded and motioned to Andrew it was time to leave.

"So, how'd it go?" Kate asked once they were in the car.

Andrew laughed. "Piece of cake. All I had to do was take out the trash, and the rest of the time I spent playing games. Had I known it would have been this easy, I would have started a long time ago."

Kate sighed in disappointment. Once again, he was getting away with the easy road, learning he did not have to be accountable for his actions. Part of her felt bad for feeling this way, but as a mom, she knew he needed something to give him a wakeup call in life.

***

Summer vacation was more hectic than Kate's regular work schedule would have been. With Megan not in school, her speech and occupational therapist came to the house several times a week to work with her. Kate ran all three of them to different therapists for coping with the initial abuse, and then there were meetings with Andrew's probation officer periodically at their home, all the while ensuring Andrew didn't miss his community service time. Ed refused to work with any agency involved in the case, so Kate took charge of filling out any paperwork needed for the county to cover the charges, and worked with Andrew's preventive care caseworker. Joe helped on his days off, but his company had issued mandatory over-time for the interim, and he was working twelve hours shifts almost daily.

Her sole focus was on getting her family back on track, yet she was wrapped so tightly within this surreal world she couldn't breathe. It was consuming her life. Her sense of obligation packed the calendar with no end in sight.

The one notion Kate could not let go of was her fear of Andrew's past behaviors, and the possibility they would one day come crashing down upon them. It was now or never to get a handle on his physical aggressions before the legal battles took another ugly turn. She researched therapists in her area that dealt with children's issues.

The Applewood Center for Children looked to be the answer. They specialized in dealing with troubled kids like Andrew. The only problem now was getting him to agree to go. Kate knew she had to be tactful in her approach or he would refuse to come. Picking up the phone, she dialed his number and nervously paced the floor while it rang.

"Hello?" Andrew answered.

"Hey. I thought I'd take you out to lunch tomorrow. They just opened a Dave & Buster's not far from your house. I heard the arcade inside there has the new pinball game you like. We could play a while after we eat." *And then drive to a new therapist.*

"Okay. I haven't had much to eat since school got out anyways. Dad's never here to cook anything."

I'm not surprised. "I'll pick you up at noon," Kate told him.

The restaurant was loud, smelled of greasy food, and was over stimulating with all the arcade games; It was the perfect distraction. Doling out all her money, Kate watched Andrew toss quarter after quarter into the slots as she sat nervously picking at her food. When their table was filled with tickets ready to be traded in for worthless prizes, Andrew exchanged his bounty for a plush parrot, then Kate ushered him into the car and drove in the opposite direction of his house.

"Where are we going?" he asked in an untrusting voice.

Kate glanced at her son then focused her eyes back on the road. "To see a new therapist," she said without taking another glimpse of his expression of the news.

"You tricked me!"

"I'm sorry. But I knew you wouldn't come willingly. Can we please just go inside and talk with this lady? I really think it will help."

Andrew shrugged his shoulders in defeat. When they arrived he got out of the car, and followed inside without a hassle. White walls, two rows of chairs, a water cooler, and outdated magazines. The ambiance was the same as any other office, more clinical than personal. Just enough of an attempt to make you feel comfortable, without overextending the welcome.

"Hello," greeted the therapist. "I'm Mindy, it's nice to meet you." She extended her hand to each of them. "I think to start off I am going to talk with just Mom first. Andrew, you can wait here and play with my dog, Muffin. She comes to work with me all the time and loves to play with the kids."

Muffin swirled around Andrew's feet in hopes of being

petted. Ignoring him, Andrew grabbed a magazine and slumped into a chair, allowing his foot to accidently-on purpose kick the dog after his mother and therapist turned to walk away. Kate was led around the corner to a small office and offered a seat. Mindy began refreshing herself on the intake paperwork Kate had previously sent to her. "Mrs. Rose, tell me why you wanted me to see your son today."

Kate couldn't help notice the family photos the therapist had sitting on her desk. She had two children herself it appeared, a boy and a girl. Both sported huge smiles, showcasing their perfectly-straight white teeth. The Stepford-looking children made her feel small. Kate shifted in her chair before sharing with the therapist her family woes. "Andrew has long history of behavioral problems. His aggressions started at age two."

"Did anything significant happen in his life around the same time?"

"His sister was born," Kate admitted, taking another jealous glance at Mindy's two darling children.

"It's not unusual for jealousy to occur when a sibling is born. What kinds of aggression have you seen?"

"He seems to have no regard for others. No regrets for the things he's done, or empathy for those he hurt." Kate found herself citing incident after incident that occurred over his short lifetime; each one just as malicious as the one prior; all meticulously planned. "Right now he is on probation for several sexual offenses and is attending sexual offender therapy. However, I feel it would be beneficial if he could have someone address his other needs."

Mindy set her papers down and slid toward the front of her seat. "What I can do is talk with Andrew over several sessions. Then I can go over my thoughts with you."

"Sounds good. There has always been a question in my mind as to whether or not he had an undiagnosed label. I'm open to any input you could give me."

"I'll do my best to get to the root of his problems. Let's go switch places and I'll bring Andrew back so we can get acquainted."

Out in the waiting room Andrew was still leafing through the magazine, looking bored. Kate sat down next to her son, noticing Muffin was hiding in the corner of the room. She walked over to the dog and scooped her into her arms while Andrew got up and traipsed back into the therapy room with Mindy.

"Nice to meet you, Andrew," she said once they were back in her office. "I have all my new clients fill out this self-assessment before we start so I can get to know them better. Do you mind filling it out?"

Andrew wrote his name on the top, skimmed the questions, and handed it back without answering a single one.

Mindy accepted the paperwork, but tried verbally probing him to gauge what his feelings were on being there. "What brings you here today?"

"My mother," he answered while staring at the ceiling.

This wasn't the first time Mindy had encountered a client who didn't want to be there. She was calm and persistent in her approach. "And why do you think she wanted you to come here?"

He shrugged. "I don't know. She thinks something's wrong with me."

"Do you think something is wrong with you?"

Andrew gave her a strange look in disbelief that she had just asked him that. "No! Why would I think something was wrong with me?"

"Do you ever have thoughts of harming yourself?" Mindy inquired.

Andrew diverted his eyes "No," he answered while slightly nodding his head yes.

Making more notes in her files, she decided to push the envelope a little farther. "Do you have thoughts of harming others?"

Andrew sat silently while crossing his arms in front of him, refusing to respond. Hoping to get more of a response, Mindy stood up to water the plants. She often found that clients were more apt to open up if someone wasn't directly looking at them. It seemed to reduce the pressure. "What do you like to do for fun?" she rattled on.

Andrew's eye followed her as she wandered around the room. He wasn't sure if he could trust her, but answered the question just the same. "Video games."

"Do take part in school activities? Perhaps participate in sports or a club?"

Andrew tightly gripped the hand rest on his chair and began tapping his feet against the floor. "Why would I do that?"

Noticing Andrew was becoming frustrated, Mindy finished puttering around the office and sat back down. "Some people find it enjoyable. They like hanging out with their friends."

"I have no friends," Andrew admitted, drooping his body down and looking embarrassed.

Mindy treaded carefully, not wanting to upset him any further. "How come?" she asked in a comforting tone.

Andrew narrowed his eyes and titled his head away from her. "Because everybody is stupid."

Knowing she just hit a nerve with Andrew, she wanted to explore the question further. "I see. Why do you think they're stupid?"

Andrew wiped his sweaty palms on his pants. "They just are," he told her. "Are we done yet?"

Mindy looked at her watch. "We do have another twenty minutes available to us, but I am not in the habit of forcing people to stay against their will.

Andrew quickly stood up and headed toward the door. "Good, I'm done then."

"I'll respect that. Let's go find your mother," Mindy suggested, escorting Andrew back out to where Kate was. He had a look of disgust on his face as he walked out of the therapy room and headed straight for the car without a word. *Some things never change.*

Kate thanked Mindy for her time, and then made another appointment for the following week. *Would Andrew come willingly or worse yet, would he tell his father she had brought him there? Ed could refuse to allow her to bring him back again.* She feared the worse, but the following Tuesday when she arrived, Andrew was in a pleasant mood when he hopped into the car.

Though he still kept his guard up, Andrew opened up slightly during his therapy session. At the end of their third visit together, Kate was invited back in for a final report.

"I spoke with some of my other colleagues about Andrew. I filled them in on his past history, and we discussed the details of my sessions with him. I'm sorry to say that everyone is in agreement. His needs are greater than what we can provide. We cannot help him here. We feel Andrew could benefit from a more intensive level of care, such as a day treatment facility. They would be able to give him more assistance in learning appropriate social behaviors."

Kate wasn't overly shocked at the news, yet at the same time, she felt somewhat validated in her concerns.

"Do you have a definitive reason for why he has been acting out?"

"It's possible he could have Oppositional Defiant Disorder or Reactive Attachment Disorder, but further testing would need to be done before a concrete diagnosis could be given."

"And the only way to get the evaluation is to put him in a treatment facility?" Kate inquired, already knowing the answer.

"I'm sorry. I wish I could do more for you. If you want, I could put you in contact with other agencies who deal with children like Andrew."

Kate shook her head in defeat. She was grateful Mindy was honest and didn't string her along, but couldn't help but to feel frustrated. There seemed nowhere for them to go to get help. The idea of simply committing her son to a facility in hopes of finding an answer was out of the question. She was going to have to find somebody willing to clinically assess him on an outpatient basis. The next morning, she placed a call to the pediatrician with her concerns and requested a referral.

"I know of a well-respected child psychiatrist I can refer him to," Dr. Sanders told Kate. "There's usually a waiting list several months long to get in, but considering his past history of physical aggression, I'll see if I can push for an expedited appointment. You won't get an immediate answer though. The intake is a three-step process. The first appointment is held between just the parents and the psychiatrist. It's probably best if you and Ed go separately. The second appointment will be with only the child. The third is held with both the parents and the child together. During the final appointment, a plan would be put in place on the best way to proceed with any new diagnosis."

"I understand, Dr. Sanders. I appreciate your help."

"I'll start the referral today. They'll let you know when a space opens up."

Kate got the phone call from the psychiatrist's office in two short weeks. They were ready to schedule Andrew's first appointment on Wednesday. The new psychiatrist requested that she prepare a detailed list of Andrew's past behaviors, and bring it with her to the first appointment.

Kate wrote two full pages on particular incidents that came to her right away. Then, she thought perhaps she was too close to the situation, so she asked family and friends for their non-biased opinions. They came up with things Kate had totally forgotten about. By the time her list for the doctor was complete, she had five pages to give to the psychiatrist.

The incidents ranged from the year when Andrew was not allowed to use the school restrooms unsupervised, to the time he had filled his aunt's brand new pool with sand and newspaper. While Kate couldn't prove Andrew had been the one to lock their cat in the closet for a week, it did seem suspicious how he knew where to find him after her own search came up empty. The worst incident had been Megan's poor bunny, Mr. Whiskers. Kate never did believe the dog had opened the rabbit's cage, killed it, skinned it, and left only a skeleton sitting out to be discovered.

Kate had blocked many of those memories until now. The list was full of behaviors not usually seen by typical children, and the more she stared at what was in front of her, the more she began to wonder: *What drives a person to do such acts?* They bordered on sociopathic tendencies.

When the doctor met with Ed, she told him about the list Kate had given her. He was furious, accusing his ex-wife of nitpicking on Andrew and trying to throw him under the bus. Ed didn't seem to care the doctor had asked her to write the list; instead, it was another reason to claim she didn't care about her son. No matter what attempts Kate made to help Andrew, Ed made it look like she was out for vengeance.

What Ed didn't understand was that Kate wasn't the only one who saw these behaviors. Everyone who came in contact with Andrew saw them as well.

CHAPTER EIGHTEEN

Play therapy proved to be very beneficial to Megan's recovery. She used stuffed animals and dolls to reenact the abuse and learned to take power from the situation. Ann taught her when she felt that she was being put in an awkward situation, she could yell NO, and then call 911 for safety. It was a good way for her to realize it was okay to not trust everybody unconditionally.

"I'm mad at you and I don't want to see you anymore," Megan said to Andrew on the pretend phone at Ann's office. She slammed the toy down as soon as the words came out, and then paused to see if she would get in trouble for being mean. When Ann commended her for being brave, Megan appeared proud. "Can I make another call?" she asked.

"Sure. Who are you going to call this time?"

"My real dad. I want to tell him I'm scared and don't want to come over any more."

Ann picked up the phone and handed it to Megan. "Why are you scared?" she asked, knowing they had hit a pivotal moment.

"Because he hurts me."

"How does he hurt you?" Ann coaxed.

Megan set the toy phone next to her as she spoke. "He rubs my belly and puts his fingers inside of me, just like this," she explained as she put her hands underneath her shirt and rubbed her chest to show Ann what her dad did to her.

"Where were you when this happened?"

"At Grandma's house. She was in the kitchen and Dad and I were watching television. Dad had the blanket over us while he did it. I'm mad at him...I don't want to see him again."

"Then let's call your father to tell him how you feel," Ann justified by handing her the pretend phone.

Megan held it to her ear and dialed three random numbers. "Dad, I don't want to spend the night with you anymore because I'm afraid you'll hurt me. And I don't want to go out to eat with you either," she blurted out then quickly hung up the phone.

Ann was quite proud of her for showing assertiveness. "How did it feel to tell your father that?" she asked.

"I'm mad at him," Megan repeated.

Ann nodded her head in agreement. "I know. Are you ready to go out and see mom now?"

"Yeah!" Megan shouted as she got to her feet.

When they came out from their session earlier than usual, Kate knew something wasn't right. Ann pulled her aside while Megan got a sticker from the receptionist. "Megan disclosed during the session that her father has been hurting her again. She even went as far as to demonstrate it for me. I'm going to place another hotline call to report it. I also want to increase my time with her. Since it's fresh in her mind, if we deal with it right away she stands a greater chance of recovering quicker."

Kate started to tear up thinking this was never going to end. Her daughter was only nine-years-old, and already forced to endure things most adults can't even cope with. Together, the mother-daughter duo walked out of the office emotionally split in two, but joined together by the hand.

When they got into the car, Kate stared at the water flowing in the river in front of her. It flowed so peacefully while she sat in a state of bitter shock and sadness. Kate longed for the days of solitude in her life. A tear trickled down her cheek for the little girl sitting next to her, who so innocently was begging for somebody to help her. Whose only wish in the world was for the bad things to stop happening to her. Wasn't that the job of her parents, to protect her from the evil in the world? How could her own father be causing her all this pain? Kate's blood raged at the thought of him doing such repulsive acts with her.

The thought of reliving another investigation and more legal battles made Kate want to hurl. It had been a very long emotional year, and her body was physically drained. She had long since given up hope that the legal system was going to protect her fragile little girl. On the drive home, she tried to occupy Megan's mind with happy thoughts. They made a list of all the things they wanted to do before summer vacation ended. Daytrips to the beach, picnics in the park, flying kites on windy days, and of course, frequent visits to the local ice cream stand; all the ordinary things that put smiles on the faces of innocent children. It sounded like heaven, if only they could get to a point in their lives when harmony would surround them.

This time it only took CPS one day before they were at the house to conduct yet another interview. "Megan, do you remember Mrs. Emmerson?" Kate asked her daughter. "She needs to talk with you again."

Kate gestured for her guest to sit in a chair, and then pulled out the one next to her for Megan to climb into.

Mrs. Emmerson flashed Megan a forced smile. "Hi, Megan. I hear you told Ann that you were mad at your dad. How come?"

"I'm mad at him," Megan blurted out, curling her knees toward her chest and sticking her fingers in her ears.

"Can you tell me why?" Mrs. Emmerson pressed, trying to take Megan's hands away from her face.

Megan pulled back, and curled up tighter. "When he gives me a bath it hurts all over. I don't want to see him."

"I see," Mrs. Emmerson rolled her eyes and turned to Kate. "Do you have another court date coming up?"

Kate bit her tongue, seething. "No," she answered with a hint of attitude. As much as Kate wanted to give Mrs. Emmerson a piece of her mind, this was not the time or place to be making a scene.

"Megan, is there any other reason you would not want to see your father anymore?"

Picking up her bear, Megan held him to her face to talk to him. "He's mean to us, and so isn't Andrew. Isn't that right, Chubbie?"

Mrs. Emmerson didn't like being ignored. She lowered Megan's bear onto her lap and looked into her eyes. "And how about your mom?" she asked. "Does she want you to see them?"

"I think she's had enough for today," Kate interrupted. "Honey, why don't you go upstairs and play now."

"Okay, Mommy," Megan replied as she ran up to her room.

Kate waited until the sound of her footsteps echoed from above, then escorted Mrs. Emmerson to the door. "She's just a little girl. Why would you do that to her?"

Mrs. Emmerson hiked her purse onto her shoulders and turned to leave. "Just trying to get to the facts, Mrs. Rose. The judge will have my report in a day or two." Mrs.

Emmerson strutted out of the house and Kate slammed the door behind her, her emotions immediately escalated.

She couldn't believe Child Protective Services thought she had coached her daughter to say something prior to a court date in order to sway the judge to her side. CPS were the ones who had told her the only way to truly know if a child was telling the truth is if they could recall the incident with the same details after a long period of time. That time had long since passed, and Megan's story had never veered from the original. *My little girl keeps repeating her story because it really happened. She is scared of her father and brother. Why has nothing been done to protect this innocent child?*

***

"There's no way I'm going to allow the police to talk with my son," Ed screamed. "I've had enough of that bitch trying to ruin his life."

Detective Hite tried to reason with Ed during the phone call. "Sir, we need a statement from him so we can clear up the new allegations."

Ed's voice grew with intensity with every word he spoke. "Nobody is going to talk to my son without a lawyer. I'm going to protect him at all cost."

"You can have your lawyer meet us at the station if you want," Detective Hite suggested.

"I'm not bringing him down to the damn station, and you're not going to interrogate him, or me."

The phone went dead, leaving the police to come up with the only other option they had. "Mrs. Rose, it's Detective Hite. We're going to need you to bring Andrew down to the station again. His father is refusing to cooperate."

"I'm not going to do it," Kate said flatly.

Detective Hite wasn't prepared for her not to cooperate. "You did it once before. We really need your help."

"I'm sorry, but it's not my responsibility to get you access to Andrew. Quite frankly, I'm tired of you doing a half-assed job investigating the case. If you need a statement, go see Andrew's probation officer." Kate hung up the phone before she said something she would later regret.

***

"Ed has been exceedingly uncooperative lately," April informed the police when they called to set up a meeting during Andrew's next visitation with her. "So I will not be alerting him of your arrival. He has missed too many scheduled appointments as it is, and if Ed even thinks something is amiss, he won't bring him in."

"Not to worry, we won't let him know we're coming. We'll see you on Tuesday."

***

The distinct sound of Ed's heavy and slow footsteps echoed down the hallway alerting the personnel of their presence. "Someone will be with you in a moment," the receptionist said glancing up from the piles of paper in front of her. Ed stared straight ahead without offering a response.

"I'll bring Andrew back into my office," April told Detective Hite after the receptionist called to say Andrew had arrived. "Once he's away from his father, you can go into the waiting room and get a statement from Ed."

"Sounds like a plan," Detective Hite agreed.

April walked out to the waiting room to bring Andrew back for his appointment. "Hi Andrew, good to see you again," she called out. "Why don't you come on back and then your dad can join us in a little bit."

Ed glared at her suspiciously before nodding to his son to follow. As soon as the door closed behind them, Detective Hite strolled out and stopped directly at Ed's feet. "Mr. Preston?"

"What do you want?" Ed asked with a hint of annoyance.

"Detective Hite," he introduced himself while extending his hand. "We've meet before."

Ed leaned back in the chair, crossing his arms on top of his portly belly. "I remember," he retorted, snubbing the hand in front of him.

"It seems your daughter has made new allegations against you, and I will need you to come with me and give a statement."

"That little bitch, April tricked me," Ed yelled, jumping to his feet. "She had no right to allow you to ambush me during my son's appointment."

"Sir, part of your son's probationary agreement is cooperating with any agency involved in his care. Since you refused to come on your own accord, we needed to find a place to conduct our interview."

Ed got real close and shook a pudgy finger at the detective's face as he yelled. "You can't talk to him without me in there. I refuse to let you," he screamed.

Detective Hite took a defensive step back and tried to remain calm. "Sir, if you come with me I will take your statement first, and when April is done talking with your son, I will bring him in with us to get his statement."

Ed clenched his jaw and snarled. "This isn't fair! My ex-wife is out to get me and will stop at nothing. This is all a farce."

"Mr. Preston, if you don't come with me now I will

have to detain you."

"You want a statement? Fine, I'll give you a statement. I want it on paper how much of a bitch Kate really is," Ed screamed as he followed Detective Hite into the next room.

"Thank you for cooperating," the detective started once they were in a private area. "What I need from you is a formal statement about the allegations your daughter has made against you. She claims you have touched her vagina while giving her a bath. What I need from you is a written response to these allegations."

Ed took the pen and paper the detective held out for him. He scribbled fast and furious, making his handwriting barely legible.

"My name is Ed Preston and I am giving this statement today to Detective Hite while at the probation department. I have been advised there are new allegations regarding me. My daughter has made accusations that I have touched her vaginal area. This is false. Megan has only been to my current resident a couple of times. Yes, I do supervise her being bathed because she needs assistance. I help her in the tub because I am concerned about her health. If I don't help, she will come out half-bathed. Megan does watch television while at my mother's house, but I never touched her under a blanket while she watched her shows. I am upset about these allegations. My ex-wife just wants Andrew to get sent away so she is making stuff up and training my daughter to repeat them. This is all I have to say at this time."

"Okay, Mr. Preston, that should do it," Detective Hite acknowledged as he signed his name as witness at the bottom of the statement. "I'll call April and ask her to bring Andrew in so he can give his statement now."

Drumming his fingers on the table, Ed fidgeted in his

seat until his son was brought in. "What did you tell her?" he demanded as Andrew sat across from him.

His eyes grew wide at the look of his father. "Nothing! All April said was the police needed a statement and to be honest with them."

"And I also reminded him that he is still on probation, and if he wants to stay out of trouble he needs to cooperate," April informed Ed.

"Okay, Andrew," Detective Hite started. "As April informed you, your sister has alleged that your father touched her while bathing and while watching television at your grandmother's. What I need from you is a statement verifying what you know of the situation."

Andrew's eye started to twitch as he passed a nervous glance at his father. The tension between the two could have been split clean down the middle.

Detective Hite passed Andrew a pen and paper. "I need you to state your name and tell me why you are here today."

Eyes diverted to the floor, Andrew took a deep breath while writing down his statement.

"My name is Andrew Preston. I don't know why my sister Megan said my father has touched her inappropriately. I usually stay in my room at my Grandma's when Megan is over and she stays downstairs to watch TV. I don't go in the bathroom when she is bathing so I don't know what goes on in there. This is all I have to say."

Andrew signed his name on the bottom of the paper and slid it across the table to Detective Hite.

"Can we go now?" Ed asked, impatiently drumming his fingers loudly across the table.

"Yes, you're free to go. It doesn't seem as if there is any evidence to support the claim, so most likely the judge will dismiss the charges," the detective informed him.

Ed grew a tight, closed-lipped smile. "Let's go," he instructed Andrew as he pulled him out of his seat by his shirt collar. "That's the last time you will ever attack us again," he screamed at April before slamming the door shut behind them.

"Do you believe them?" Detective Hite asked April as they walked back down the hall to her office.

"I don't believe anything Ed says, but unfortunately Megan's statement won't hold up on her own."

CHAPTER NINETEEN

State laws were designed to protect the innocent and the weak, but Kate quickly learned there were serious flaws in the ways the justice system actually worked, and whom it really protected.

Soon she was back in court again, in hopes of modifying the visitation agreement in light of the new allegations against Ed. Kate worried what would happen if the judge didn't agree to stop Megan's visitations with her father. She had gone through so much in her young life, and it started to take a toll on her. Kate had noticed small changes in her daughter's behavior over the past few months, and it saddened her to think about the mental turmoil she must be going through. She said a silent prayer as she sat in the courtroom, asking for a guardian angel to watch over the day's events, and save her from any future peril.

Judge Lagoe entered the room and began the proceedings by reading off the new accusations against Ed. After the police report was cited, he turned to Ed and asked, "What do you have to say about these allegations?"

Ed stood up from his seat, puffed out his chest, and stared at Kate. "This is a total lie made up by my ex-wife to get me into trouble and to keep me away from my daughter."

"Sit down, Mr. Preston," the judge ordered. "I read the report from Child Protective Services after they conducted an interview with Megan. They feel her mom has been coaching her to say she had been abused in order to gain full custody of her."

Ed leaned over to where Andrew was sitting and whispered something into his ear. The satisfactory smile on both their faces was enough to make Kate nauseous.

"It is their opinion that the case be dropped, and visitation between child and father remain status quo," the judge concluded.

In the minds of the authorities, Kate was nothing more than a vindictive mother trying to get full custody of her daughter by fabricating a story. She was outraged. *How could someone think I would train my little girl to say disgusting things had happened to her? Did they truly believe I also showed her how to demonstrate these actions to keep her father away? If I had coached her into saying things that weren't true so I could have her to myself, then I'd be as guilty of taking advantage of her fragile state as they had. I could never do that to anyone, let alone my own child.*

Kate knew Megan was incapable of being coached. Now she had only a few precious moments to prove it to the people who controlled the fate of her future.

Ed's lawyer, Mr. Zimmerman, immediately requested the court dismiss the new restraining order petition that Kate had filed against his client.

"Request granted," echoed into Kate's ears as her heart sank deep inside of her chest.

Kate tried to explain to the judge that what CPS had seen was due to Megan's language deficit, not any deception on her part, and begged him to take Megan's disability into consideration. Because she had been so meticulous on pinpointing the IEP goals to them, they misconstrued it as a sign of her being deceitful. Kate didn't know what to do. She had worked so hard to make sure everyone understood her daughter's ability level, and they accused her of fabricating a story for her benefit. It was clear to Kate now the court was trying to protect Ed's parental rights, instead of Megan's civil rights of being safe.

She knew she couldn't persuade the judge to consider her petition, but hoped maybe he would at least consider an alternative option. "Would you consider granting Megan supervised visitations with her father given the extent of all the allegations that have been made?"

The judge seemed exhausted at the ongoing trial. "Why do you feel supervised visitations are necessary Ma'am?"

"Because my daughter is afraid to be alone with her father. If somebody was with them, then there will be no room for error as to what happens when they are together. It's only protecting everyone's interest."

"I am not granting supervised visitations, Mrs. Rose."

"Then will you please hold off on making a final determination on visitations until after a statement can be made from Megan's therapist since she was the one who placed the hotline call in the first place?"

"Very well. We will meet again in two weeks and my final decision will be made then."

As soon as Kate got home from the courthouse, she was on the phone with Ann.

"Ann, it's Kate. Things didn't go well in court today. The judge denied my request to vacate the visitation order and even ruled against supervised visitations."

"Even after I placed the hotline call?" she gasped.

"Child Protective Services wrote in their report that I was coaching Megan to say those things."

"That's outrageous. Even if you wanted to coach Megan to say something, she doesn't have the capacity to retain an untrue story. The details of the abuse would have gotten lost in translation."

"I know, but the judge is taking Child Protective's word over mine. He agreed on holding off for two weeks before making a final decision. Do you think you can talk with Child Protective Services and explain to them what Megan disclosed during her therapy session?"

"I'm going to call them right now. I'll get back to you."

Ann hung up the phone and immediately dialed Mrs. Emmerson. "Do you realize," Ann stressed, "that Megan has not changed her story one bit over the course of time I have known her? She clearly states her dad had touched her butt and belly, which is her word for her chest, just like Andrew had been doing to her, and reports she does not want to visit with either of them anymore."

"Do you think maybe Megan is making things up just to get them into trouble and to save herself from having to see them again?"

"Are you kidding me? That's not even possible. Megan has a severe inability to rationalize cause and effect situations. She doesn't even realize that by her telling what happened caused all of this legal drama and could affect her visitation schedule with her father."

"Well, I'm sorry Ann, but with the limited statements Megan has provided, nothing else can be done. Even if I did believe her, she would not be a reliable witness in the courtroom, so prosecution of the case would be hard."

"I understand why you don't feel comfortable with putting Megan on the stand, but I am going to put something in writing for the judge before the next court date. I firmly believe Megan is telling the truth."

"Do what you need to do. I'm standing behind my report."

Ann hung up the phone and immediately called Kate back. "Kate, I just spoke with Mrs. Emmerson. She's not going to retract her statement."

"So the judge is going to think I'm coaching my daughter? That's absurd," she protested.

"It's not that much of a setback. I'm going to send the judge a copy of my office notes. I've had more contact with Megan than CPS has, so my statement should weigh a little heavier than theirs."

"Thanks, Ann. I still wish there was more I could do to help the case."

"There is one more option available to you; a way to prove to the court that Megan was telling the truth without using words at all. We could use physical evidence. The Child Advocacy Center works with children who have been sexually abused and provides them with a trauma exam in a friendly atmosphere. It would be similar to the exam she had at the hospital, but this time it would be videotaped and photographs would be taken in case anything showed up that could be used as evidence in court. Would you like me to set up an appointment for you?"

"I hate to put her through anything else, but it seems like I have no other option. Megan needs to be protected."

"I'll call them now and put in the referral. They'll be in touch with you."

***

The first thing Megan noticed when they walked into the Child Advocacy Center was the mural on the wall.

Three of the walls had a light blue background, with colorful fish swimming about. Ripples in the water had been painted in to make the fish appear to be moving, and just a hint of the sun's rays cast down into the water. The scene was both entrancing and calming.

"Welcome," a young woman with long blonde hair greeted as they signed in at the front desk. "My name is Julia and I will be one of the nurses helping you today. It's nice to meet you both."

Megan hid behind her mother and squeezed her hand tight. Kate allowed her gaze to briefly meet Julia's warm smile before prying Megan out from under her.

"Let me give you a tour of the place before we start. That way it will be more comfortable for Megan," Julia suggested.

"That would be nice," Kate answered.

After Julia showed them around she brought Megan into the examination room. Once again, Megan changed into a gown and hopped onto the table while Kate helped her get her feet up into the stirrups. The nurses were wonderful, talking softly to her through every step so she knew ahead of time what was going on.

It was hard for Kate watching her daughter having to be so vulnerable. She found herself having to turn away as one nurse held her legs apart while another snapped pictures of her private areas. Megan was very apprehensive, but cooperative throughout. She had already gone through so much and had been braver than Kate could have thought possible given the situation. As proud as Kate was that Megan was so strong, a tear ran down her face as she wished her daughter didn't have to be.

As soon as the nurses finished the testing, Kate helped Megan get dressed again so she could regain the dignity she had just lost, then lead her out to the front room. The receptionist flashed Megan a smile and asked if she wanted to pick out a stuffed animal and a book to take home for her courage.

"Go ahead and pick something, honey," Kate told her. "I'm going to talk with the nurse while you're looking."

A small grin crept up on Megan's face as she walked over to the bin and looked at the different colored teddy bears that were inside.

"What did the test results show?" Kate asked one of the nurses as soon as Megan was out of earshot.

"There was some tearing in her, but it could be the result of constipation. There is no way for us to prove it was caused from an injury. Even if we could show there was physical evidence of trauma, there would be no way to prove who did it to her," the nurse gently explained.

As true as that was, any shred of evidence showing she had internal injuries might be enough to put doubt in the judge's mind about who had caused it, and this might be enough to grant the petition to keep her away from Ed and Andrew, and out of harm's way. While she thanked God Megan sustained no physical injuries, Kate also found herself cursing that once again they lacked any proof they needed to get an Order of Protection.

Joe was stuck at work the day they were to return to court, which left Karen to be Kate's support person. Together the friends walked in, neither of them expecting a good outcome. *Will this be the time my daughter finally gets her voice heard or will it once again be dismissed and she would be forced to go back to a place where she was unsafe?*

Kate held her breath as Judge Lagoe began speaking. "I received a letter from Ann at Counseling and Psychological Services. In her professional opinion, Megan is not capable of being coached and she believes Megan has sustained significant emotional distress by being with her father. Therefore, I am throwing out the previous CPS report that states mom has been coaching her."

Thank You, Ann! Kate closed her eyes, held her breath, and anxiously awaited to hear the rest of Megan's fate.

"I am issuing a temporary no-contact order between Megan and her father. The mother's rights with both of the children will remain unchanged."

Karen hugged Kate tight as relief washed over her. She couldn't wait until Megan came home from school to tell her the good news.

Ed stood up from his seat and started cursing at Kate from across the room. "How dare you, you little bitch. You think you can take my daughter away from me?"

"Counsel, control your client or he will be removed," instructed the judge.

Ed relented and sat down, but his eyes still threatened his ex-wife from across the room. Kate refused to look in his direction and stared straight ahead for the remainder of the proceedings. After the judge dismissed them, Kate hung back in the hallway to talk with her lawyer, Mrs. Jackson, before leaving.

"You won't always be there to protect her," Ed screamed at Kate's attorney as he passed by her in the hall. "And make no mistake; I will come after that fucking bitch."

"Mr. Preston, if you cannot control yourself I will have you held in contempt for threatening my client," Mrs. Jackson warned, sheltering Kate behind her.

"You better watch your back, Kate," Ed threatened as he shook off the bailiff who tried to restrain him.

"Do you want to press harassment charges?" Mrs.

Jackson asked after Ed was escorted out of the building.

"No," Kate said. "He's not worth my time."

"You really should, Kate," she persisted.

Kate shook her head and tossed one hand in the air. "It's okay, I'm used his threats."

"Well, I'm going to go let the judge know what just happened. It will look more favorable to your case the next time you appear. In the meantime, go home and stay safe."

The courts had thrust their authority over Ed, and he waged a personal war back against each of the agencies involved in Andrew's care. First, he refused to cooperate with any request from the preventive care caseworker, the probation department, and Andrew's therapist. Then, he began to threaten the caseworkers, both on the phone, and in person. Several times he even kicked a few of them out of his house when they came to do their home visits. Each time Ed did not get his own way, he called up the agency supervisor and requested a new worker for the case. This bought him extra time before the department caught on to his tricks.

While Kate wasn't surprised by any of this, she didn't understand how he did not get it through his head that these people were in his life because his son needed help. Ed played the system well, but it was catching up with him. Probation grew tired of dealing with him and called Kate to see if she would petition the court to gain back custody of Andrew, in order for him to get the care he needed.

As much as Kate knew her son needed the recommended services, she wasn't sure how she would be able to have him back in the house permanently ever again. Before she made such a drastic decision, Kate knew she would have to discuss it with Andrew's psychologist at his next appointment. It was only a week away and she didn't want to make any life-altering decisions until she had a chance to discuss her findings on his mental health status.

CHAPTER TWENTY

August 2001

Megan and Kate tried hard to enjoy their last few weeks of summer vacation before the start of the new school year. The pressure of the last six months had left them drained, and in need of relaxation.

Megan pumped her legs harder and harder, laughing as she tried to swing high enough to reach the sky from her swing set. Kate sat in a chair in front of her, reading a book while sipping on ice-cold lemonade. The sound of the phone ringing from the house interrupted their quiet world.

"Hello," Kate answered, surprised to find Andrew on the other end.

"Hey, can I come over and swim?" he asked.

Baffled, she hesitated for a second. *That's a little strange. He never calls wanting to come over.* "I guess. Joe's working out of town and your sister is playing outside. It'll take me a few minutes to get her into the car. Make sure you're ready when I get there."

"Okay," he agreed.

Kate hung up the phone and sighed. The afternoon had been quiet and peaceful. She knew once Andrew came all that would end. She picked up Megan's shoes from the ground and tickled her toes as they swung toward her. Once she slowed down enough, Kate grabbed both her legs until she came to a complete stop and slipped her sandals onto her feet.

"What'cha stop me for?" she asked with a sour-puss face.

Kate buckled up her daughter's shoes then playfully tapped her button-shaped nose with one finger. "We're going to pick your brother up so he can come over and swim," she answered.

"Do we have to?" Megan whined.

"It's a beautiful day and Andrew wants to swim in the pool. Besides, I'm sure he misses seeing us. Now go hop in the car so we can get right back for you to play."

"Fine," she complained and stomped off.

Kate grabbed her keys from the house, and then joined Megan in the car. "Ready to go, Puddin'?"

"No," Megan pouted.

"Let's play 'I Spy' on the way over," Kate suggested.

"Okay!" she squealed with a huge grin on her face.

Kate started the car, glanced around to find an object, then looked in the rearview mirror at her daughter. "I spy, with my little eye, something blue," she declared as she backed out of the driveway.

Megan scanned the car for something that matched the blue color. "Is it my doll's shirt?" she asked, holding it up for her mother to see.

Kate shook her head. "Nope, try again."

Moving her eyes from one thing to another, she finally tugged on her mother's sleeve. "Your shirt?"

Kate reached back and high-fived her daughter. "You got it! Now it's your turn to choose a color."

"I chose pink," she cheered.

"Remember the rules; you have to say I spy with my little eye, something pink."

"Oh, yeah," she said scrunching up her face recalling how to play the game. "I spy with my little eye something pink."

"Is it your shirt?" Kate laughed.

Megan giggled. "Yes! You're so smart, Mommy." By the time they reached the house, Megan had won four out of the five games.

When Kate pulled into Ed's driveway, Andrew was nowhere in sight. Impatiently, Kate honked the horn. Andrew emerged at the door for only a minute, then disappeared back inside. When he didn't come back out, Kate turned off the car and went to the front door. The sound of Ed screaming from inside flooded through the screen windows. *What are they fighting about now?* Not up to dealing with any of the drama, Kate considered hopping back into the car to head home, but curiosity got the best of her. She knocked on the door to find out what was going on.

When Andrew answered, she could tell they had been fighting for a while because she used to have the same look on her face every time Ed went after her. Andrew peered at his mother through the screen door.

"I'm not coming," he coldly informed her and walked away.

Kate's nerves shot right over the top. "How dare you call and expect me to drop everything to rush over here to pick you up, and then you refuse to come? I'm not playing a game here, Andrew."

"I'm not either," he retorted in a snotty tone.

Fed up, Kate turned to walk away, then stopped mid-stride. *I remember how I used to wish for someone to come to my rescue when Ed was fighting with me. I can't*

12

leave him here like this.

She went in the door without knocking. Ed and Andrew were at a standoff. Neither one looked ready to back down from the other.

"Go get in the car," Kate instructed Andrew as she shot Ed a disgusted look. Andrew darted his eyes from his father to his mother, then walked to the car and climbed in the front seat. Kate followed and slammed the door behind her.

"What on earth was that about?" Kate asked as she pulled out of the driveway.

His voice was huffy as he answered, "Nothing."

"Come on, I just saw you and your father about to kill one another. Don't tell me that was nothing."

"Can we just forget about it?" he asked.

"No. Forty minutes ago, you were in a good mood and wanted to come for a swim. Now I find you ready to take part in World War III. What gives?"

Andrew adjusted the radio dial to a hip-hop station and turned up the music to drown out the sound of his mother's voice. Kate dropped the subject and continued driving in silence.

The sun was still radiating when they got home. The three of them changed into swimsuits and headed straight for the pool. Once Andrew hit the water, he seemed to have forgotten about the fight with his father. The next hour they all swam, played Marco Polo, and showed off their diving skills. Eventually, the sound of growling stomachs forced Kate to get out and start dinner. The smell of sizzling hot dogs on the grill filled the air as the kids drip-dried in the sun. They were actually having fun, like the old days when they lived together as a family. It had been so long since there was peace among them all, Kate almost forgot what it had been like.

After dinner, the kids went back into the water to play. Being waterlogged, Kate said she would watch them while cutting the grass in the small fenced in area around the pool. Andrew grabbed the Styrofoam noodles, threw them in, and did a belly flop onto them. Megan inched her way down the ladder, easing herself into the water as usual. Kate watched them do tricks and splash one another as the lawn mower circled the pool.

Halfway through the yard, the mower sputtered and eventually ceased power. Climbing off the seat, Kate raised the hood and peered inside at the empty gas tank. Looking toward the garage where the gas can was, then back again at the kids, she couldn't decide what to do. She didn't want to walk around the back yard to get to the garage because she wouldn't be able to see what the kids were doing. Her earlier pleas to the judge came racing back.

"It would be unrealistic to think somebody could keep their eyes on a child every minute of the day. Any time I used the restroom, took a bath, or slept at night the kids would technically be unsupervised. It only takes a few moments for something to happen."

This certainly was one of those times she had been talking about. How could she go about with routine life while keeping her eyes on a child at all times? Kate hesitated a moment longer before convincing herself if the judge felt it was safe to have them together, she could take a few minutes to grab a gas can.

Taking the shortest route possible to the garage, she quickly grabbed the container, and returned to the backyard. Within five minutes, the mower was refueled and ready to pick up where she left off. As she mowed the yard around the pool, Kate noticed Megan was pushed up against the pool wall facing her, with Andrew directly behind her. They were no longer swimming around freely, but both walked around the perimeter of the pool, in sync with the lawnmower.

They kept perfect pace with their mother as she mowed, and mimicked her every move, forward or backward. They never went on a side of the wall she wasn't on, nor were they really playing anymore, just following Kate's movements. Andrew waved a couple of times, flashing a cunning smile every so often. Kate waved back with a puzzled look on her face. Something wasn't quite right, but she couldn't put her finger on it. She could see them, from the neck up anyway, and nothing appeared out of the ordinary. Still, Kate couldn't settle the odd feeling growing inside of her.

She decided to shut the mower off. As if on cue, both the kids got out of the water without a word and dried off. "Why are you getting out? I was getting ready to hop back in and play," Kate told them.

Andrew hung his towel on the fence to dry. "I don't want to play anymore."

"Me either," repeated Megan.

"Okay. If you're all done for the night, then I want you both to change out of your wet clothes," Kate instructed.

"Can I watch T.V.?" Megan asked quietly.

Kate took her daughter's wet towel out of her hand. "Sure sweetie, after you put on something dry."

Megan changed her clothes then sat on the floor in front of the television lining up her toys in neat rows. Kate cleaned up the dinner dishes, but couldn't shake off the distinct quietness between the two kids. Something told her it was time to take Andrew back to Ed's house.

After Megan's shower that evening, they played a board game and read a bedtime story together. Kate placed a kiss upon Megan's forehead and tucked her snug into her bed. Kate's head hit the pillow not long after that.

Eight o'clock the next morning, Megan climbed into her mother's bed and woke her up. "Morning, honey," Kate greeted tiredly.

Megan's voice trembled as she whispered into her mother's ear, "Andrew touched me again."

Kate bolted up in panic. "When?"

"While we were watching you mow the lawn," she whispered.

It all made sense now. Andrew had made sure they were always on the same side of the pool as the riding lawn mower. He was smart enough to figure out if they had they been on an opposite wall, she would have seen what he was doing.

Kate's stomach churned. What kind of sick person would molest someone right in front of his own mother? He had been staring right at her! Sadly enough, Kate wasn't shocked this time; she was simply enraged. This was beyond defiance, and she was pretty sure it was all about power.

Kate was suddenly caught in a battle of ethics. As an employee of the school district, the state recognized her as a mandated reporter. She was obligated by law to call in any suspected child abuse. Failure to do so put her at risk of being charged with a misdemeanor and subject to criminal penalties, along with having her license revoked. The law did not make any exclusion if the children involved were her own or not. This did not make the decision any easier. The first time Andrew hurt Megan, she took her to the emergency room, and they had been the ones who placed the call. Now it was all on her, and she had to do what was morally right.

"Puddin', go upstairs and check on Chubbie while Mommy makes a phone call," she instructed Megan.

"Okay, Mommy," she said, slowly making her way out of her mother's bedroom. Kate took a deep breath and picked up the phone.

"911, what's your emergency?"

Kate nervously smoothed out the blanket in front of her as she spoke. "My daughter was sexually abused," she answered.

The sound of the intake call being typed into the computer system echoed through the phone. "How old is your daughter, Ma'am?"

"She's nine."

"And she told you she had been abused?" Choking back the tears, Kate managed to respond with a quiet yes.

"Do you know who abused her?"

"Yes," she breathed. "Her brother did. He has a record of past sexual abuse already in the system."

There was a hesitation in her voice as she questioned Kate. "If you knew he has a past history then why were they allowed to be together?"

"This has been something I've been battling the courts with. Andrew was mandated by the judge to have visitations with his sister. We are heading over to the sheriff's office right now to file a new report. Can you please notify them that we are coming so they can be prepared?"

"Yes, Ma'am, I can. How soon can you be there?"

"We're on our way now," she said hanging up. Kate took a moment to try and absorb it all in. Why was this happening again? Needing her husband, she picked the phone back up and dialed Joe's cell number.

"Hi, honey, how are my two favorite girls doing?"

Kate's lips primed, the words almost too unfathomable to speak. She sucked back the tears that had dripped down her face and professed, "Joe, he did it again."

"What?" he exploded. "Kate, exactly what happened?"

She spoke in a hoarse whisper. "He called yesterday and asked to come over to swim. Then this morning, Megan says he touched her while they were in the pool."

"Oh my God, that poor girl. Have you notified the authorities?"

Kate drew in a long breath. "Yes, we're on our way to the police station now."

"I'm going to tell my boss I have an emergency and ask if I can get back home early. I may not be able to get there until tomorrow though."

"I don't know how much more I can take," Kate sobbed.

"Call me when you get home from the police station. I'll be home as soon as I can. I love you guys."

"Love you, too," she reminded him before hanging up. Kate grabbed their shoes then headed out the door without even changing out of their pajamas.

The two sat in silence the entire ride. There would have been nothing Kate could have said to her daughter to ease her pain, and the promise she had made to her to keep her safe was unintentionally broken. *Why are we were driving to the police station? Nothing had been done about the situation any other time we've been there. I don't expect the results to be any different this time.* The sad truth was they were alone in this battle, alone to fight the justice system for both protection and vindication.

Kate took her time getting out of the car after they arrived, as to preserve the last few moments of tranquility before their lives were turned upside down again. As she took Megan's hand and walked down the corridor to give their statement, one of the deputies recognized them and called to get Andrew's past records. Megan climbed onto her mother's lap as they sat in front Detective Hite's desk.

"Mrs. Rose, what brings you in today?" he asked, already knowing the information that the 911 call center had supplied him with.

Kate finger combed her daughter's hair to distract herself from the shame of reliving the events. "Andrew touched her again last night."

One eyebrow raised above the other, Detective Hite turned to Megan to hear her version of the events. "Can you tell me what happened, Megan?"

"Andrew touched my front butt," she muttered. "Not my back butt that my dad touched before. Just my front butt. Then he touched my chest."

Detective Hite put his elbow on the desk and rubbed his chin. "Where were you when he touched your front butt?"

"In the swimming pool," Megan explained.

"Was your bathing suit on or off when it happened?"

Megan looked down at the floor and studied her feet as she rhythmically swung them back and forth as she sat. "On," she told Detective Hite.

"How did he touch you then?" he asked, doubting the story was true.

Megan tightened the muscles in her face and stared straight at him. "He pulled it out and put his hands down there, just like this," she explained as she sat in her chair and went to show him. Kate had to pull her daughter's hand back before she got her pants down to demonstrate.

Detective Hite shook his head and continued with his questioning. "Where was your mom when this happened?"

"Mowing the lawn. We were watching her."

"You were watching your mom when it happened?"

he asked in surprise.

Megan nodded her head then curled her knees up and hid her face in-between them. Kate reached over and tried to soothe her by stroking her back.

Detective Hite turned to Kate. "If she could see you when it was happening, then how did you not know it was going on?"

"It's an above ground pool. I could only see them from the neck up while I was mowing the lawn."

"Didn't she say anything to you while it was happening or last night before bed?"

"No, she did not, but when she woke up this morning it was the first words out of her mouth."

Detective Hite twirled his pen in between his fingers. "Well, I don't understand. How come last time when it happened she told you right away and this time she waited until the next day?"

"I can't tell you why she waited until this morning to tell me, it's just what she did. Autistic kids sometimes can be unpredictable. But the point is she did tell, and now I want to know what you're going to do about it."

"You knew he had abused her once before, why would you continue to let him be around her?"

"I applied for an Order of Protection," Kate sternly reminded him. "And not only was it denied, but the judge is forcing them to be together. Had it been my choice, any visitations between the two of them would have ceased months ago."

Detective Hite jotted down notes in his pad, paused, then tapped his pen against his temple in thought. "What was she wearing in the pool, a one or two-piece swimsuit?"

Kate glared at him. "It was a two-piece suit, but with a surfer- style top so it would cover her entire chest. The neckline was as tall as a turtleneck and it had short sleeves. It was not revealing in any way," she clamored defensively.

"I will have somebody go talk to Andrew, but I doubt if he will confess this time. It will most likely end up being his word against hers, and because of her disability, the courts will not consider her as a reliable witness."

Kate felt a numb sensation in the pit of her stomach. *Just because she has a disability didn't mean my daughter doesn't know what happened to her. Why doesn't she ever have a voice? She is a human being and deserves the right to be protected like everyone else. The authorities knew Andrew had already done this to her once, so why is it so hard for them to believe it happened again?* She was so angry she took Megan's hand and left without saying another word. Kate knew if she opened her mouth again, she would end up saying something she would later regret.

By the time Kate pulled back into her driveway, the all-too-familiar tears started rolling down her face. Megan and Kate traipsed inside and got dressed for the day. Megan pushed the waffles around her breakfast plate. Kate cut hers into minuscule pieces, but neither one of them put a bite into their mouths. Kate replayed the scenes in her mind, trying to make sense of it. Hide and seek—abuse. Swimming—abuse. Anger—abuse. Her fork fell to the floor.

Both times Andrew had abused his sister, he'd been visibly upset prior to the incidents. Did the fights he had with his father have some kind of connection to the reason why he was sexually abusing Megan? Most rape cases are not about the sex itself, but about power and control. Having witnessed the altercation between him and his father, it would make sense he would have the need to take some control back in his own life.

***

"Your sister claims you touched her while in the swimming pool the other day. Do you want to tell me what happened?" Detective Hite asked Andrew.

April shot him a knowing look from her desk. If he wanted to abide by his probation agreement, he was to cooperate and answer all questions.

"I don't know what she's talking about," he muttered. "All we did was swim and eat dinner. My mom cut the lawn, then brought me back home."

"Did you look down your sister's bathing suit while in the pool?" April asked.

"No," he denied while shoving his hands deep inside his pockets.

She took a mental note of his shifty eye contact. "Why do you think Megan would be saying you did?"

"I don't know," Andrew shrugged.

"All right, I think we're done here," Detective Hite concluded, closing his notepad. "I'll let your dad know you're free to go." He passed a copy of his statement over to April on his way out the door. On the bottom he had scribbled, *Andrew is not the type of kid to force himself onto somebody.* April glanced at the paper and rolled her eyes.

***

"Not the type to force himself onto somebody, are you kidding me?" Kate exploded as April showed her the paper the following week. "It's in his police record that he confessed to abusing Megan before, not to mention he also admitted to abusing T.J. for over a period of a year and a half," she stammered.

"I know," April agreed. "But I can't change the detective's statement."

The drumming headache behind her temples was increasingly sharp by now. "Is he trying to say neither of them had been forced upon and it was all consensual?" Kate asked.

"I don't know what the detective was implying. I will be writing up my own statement stating that I think Andrew did hurt Megan, and I'll pass it along to Judge Lagoe."

"So what are we supposed to do now?"

"Increase Megan's therapy sessions and try not to stress too much until you get back to court. I will increase my visitations with Andrew in the meantime and see what I can do about getting him a higher level of therapy."

"What type of higher level?"

"I'd like to see it increased to several times a week. I'm also going to recommend one-on-one counseling instead of group therapy."

"Wouldn't this be a good time to reconsider the inpatient facility?" Kate urged. She knew that was what the Applewood Center had advised, and as long as she wasn't making the decision for it to happen, her conscience would be clear.

"That's a decision for the judge to make. I'll call Jolene right now and make sure she schedules Andrew accordingly. Why don't you go home and try to relax a little? We'll be in touch soon."

Kate nodded a goodbye as April cradled the phone between her shoulder and ear, flipping through her Rolodex for Jolene's number.

"Second Chances, how can I help you?"

"Jolene? It's Officer April Monet, how are you?"

"I'm good, and yourself?"

"Actually, I'm a little frustrated, that's why I'm calling. When was Andrew Preston's last therapy session?"

"He was supposed to have one last week, but never showed up. I called his father and left a message saying I had rescheduled him for this coming Friday. Why?"

"Another accusation of sexual abuse has been reported I would like you to increase his therapy and move him from a group setting to one-on-one counseling."

Jolene let out a throaty guffaw. "Andrew's been just fine during his sessions. He now participates in group discussions and agrees with all my suggestions on how to alter his behaviors. I see no reason to change anything."

"Well, a new police report would indicate otherwise, Ms. Hilton."

"And I suppose the report was filed by Andrew's mother?" she stated rather than asked. "You know that woman likes to make her son look like a monster. Ed has attended several meeting with Andrew and has filled me in on the things his ex-wife has said about her son."

April could barely contain herself. "Mrs. Rose has proven herself to be a logical and concerned mother. She has been advocating for both her children throughout all of this. So yes, when she filed another complaint, I am taking it seriously. Are you or aren't you going to increase Andrew's therapy until a judge has ordered otherwise?"

"No, I am not. As his therapist, I will decide on his level of care."

"Very well then," April intoned, hanging up the phone. She immediately turned on her computer screen and lodged a formal complaint against the agency. *What kind of professional doesn't recognize when a problem has occurred? Under my watch, child abusers are monitored carefully, and I intend to keep it that way,* she thought to herself as she finished typing out the online form. As soon as she hit submit, she pulled up a blank word document and typed a letter to her client.

Dear Andrew Preston,

As you know, another complaint has been filed against you for sexual misconduct while you are still on probation. This has prompted my request for an increase in your therapy level and an updated sexual offender assessment. I must inform you that a complaint has been filed against Second Chances Therapeutic Services and you will no longer be able to use this company to complete your probationary agreement. A list of approved therapists is enclosed. Please select one and submit proof of your first appointment within two weeks.

Sincerely,
Officer April Monet
cc: Judge Lagoe
cc: Edward Preston
cc: Kate Rose

***

I hate myself for allowing the judge to intimidate me into having the kids together again. Had I stuck to my instincts and kept them apart, no matter what the outcome, Megan wouldn't have gotten hurt again. It would have been worth going to jail over it if he wanted to hold me in contempt. Kate was still mentally berating herself as she walked through the door at home. She set her purse on the table and headed toward Andrew's bedroom. *I spent so much time and effort rebuilding him a place in my home, and instead of him appreciating it, he betrayed my trust again.*

A feeling of déjà vu fell upon her. Kate tore apart Andrew's bed, took the mattress to the garage, and carried the trashcan back into the room. Legos and action figures filled it to the top. When the room was bare, she scanned the perimeter to see if she had missed anything. Andrew's computer desk was the only thing standing between the memories she needed to escape and her sanity. Wiping the sweat from her brow, she went to unplug the computer, then paused as her hand neared the outlet, and placed it on the computer mouse instead.

Start>System tools>Browsing history> Recent Google search results
    -Girls
    -Boobs
    -Cartoon sex
    -Naked girls
    -Sex
    -Sexy girls

Disgusted, Kate ripped the plug from the wall. Her chest rose and fell at an alarming rate. *He's unbelievable. Obviously whatever he's learning in therapy is not working.* Immediately, she dialed April.

"This is Probation Officer April. Please leave a detailed message and your call will be answered within twenty-four hours. Thank You."

Kate inhaled deeply and slowly released the air through her nose while waiting for the beep. "April, it's Kate. I wanted you to know I found pornographic material on Andrew's computer. I'm really concerned. If you haven't talked to Jolene yet, could you let her know? I thought she might want to discuss it with him during his next therapy lesson. Give me a call and I'll fill you in on the details."

Kate's right hand feverishly rubbed her temple while her left hung up the phone. *I'd better let Ed know so he can check his own computer at home.*

"So the kid was looking at pictures of girls," Ed laughed when Kate called him. "What kid doesn't?"

"Kids who are in sexual offender counseling should not be looking at pornography," she reminded him.

"Why don't you stop picking on your son for every little thing and start to realize boys will be boys."

"Ed, this should not be taken lightly, especially in the face of another abuse investigation."

"It's not that big of a deal, Kate."

"Yes it is!" she screamed into the phone.

"I've had it with you getting on his case about everything," Ed berated. "Get a life."

Kate slammed the phone down. It was obvious there would be no reasoning with him. He viewed his son as perfect; she saw too many red flags that she couldn't overlook. They were at an impasse.

"What am I going to do?" Kate asked Joe in bed that evening. "How can I possibly keep fighting for both the kids when Ed blocks me every step of the way?"

"I wish I knew what to tell you, honey. The situation is horrible. I know you only want what's best for them both."

"Which seems impossible to do," Kate pointed out.

"Mommy!" Megan screamed.

Kate ran through the dark house, up to her daughter's room, and found her shaking with fear. She scooped her up and cradled her daughter in her arms. Megan had another nightmare, wet the bed again, and was soaked in her own fears. Only nine-years-old and afraid of hide-and-seek, dresses, and swimming pools.

Kate mixed up a new potion of Ann's "magic dust" and handed it to Megan. She spritzed her room in an effort to protect herself from harm. Kate wished she could spray it around their whole world.

CHAPTER TWENTY-ONE

September 2001

"Is there life outside of these four walls?" Kate asked Joe as they sat once again at the prosecutor's table, ready to hear what the judge had to say about the new allegations against Andrew.

He put his arm around his wife, and pulled her in until her lead lay upon his shoulder. "I know it hasn't been easy the past few months, but all this will eventually pass. Right now you need to concentrate on keeping Megan safe, and getting Andrew the help he needs."

Finding comfort in his arms, she buried her head deeper into them. "I don't know how much more I can take." It was reassuring to know her husband was by her side, yet their lives seemed to be in a downward spiral. Kate was thankful to have been blessed by having such a strong man in her life willing to stand by her during this difficult time.

"Court is now in session," the bailiff called. "The honorable Judge Lagoe, presiding."

"Docket # 44382, the State vs. Andrew Preston," the judge began. "Andrew is a twelve-year-old juvenile who is accused of sexual abuse for the second time in six months. Does the prosecution have any opening remarks?"

"Yes, your honor," the state attorney started. "In light of the new allegations while the child is still on probation, we move to expedite the proceedings and request that Andrew be sent to an inpatient facility for sexual offender treatment."

"How does the defense feel about this?" asked the judge.

Andrew's attorney rose. "Your honor, what we have here is a case of he said/she said. The accuser is a nine-year-old autistic child with limited cognitive abilities. There has been no substantial evidence of abuse, and my client denies any wrongdoing. I move to dismiss the current charges."

Judge Lagoe leafed through the thick pile of papers in front of him. "Without a confession from the defendant, the lack of evidence in this case gives me no option but to dismiss the accusations. However, I am concerned about what I am hearing. Therefore, I am ordering psychological testing for Andrew and mandating the request made by Andrew's probation officer to get an updated sexual offender evaluation from one of the recommended therapist. If the assessment shows he is at high-risk of re-offending, then we may need to consider a different level of care for him. As of now, both the evaluations can be done in an out-patient setting."

For the first time in months, Ed's face appeared to look worried. Andrew's lawyer whispered something into his ear, and Ed nodded while staring Kate down from across the room.

"Mr. Preston," the judge addressed Ed, "for now I am going to leave your son in your continued care. Andrew's preventive care caseworker will be keeping close tabs on him. I trust you will follow through with my directions and get the assessments completed as soon as possible. Andrew's probation officer reports that as of date you have not complied with her request. She will be expecting the reports so she can pass them along to me."

"Yes, Sir," Ed seethed through a fake smile.

"Very well. Court is adjourned."

Joe squeezed his wife's hand gently. "Let's go."

Kate let him lead her out to the car. "When? When will it all end?" she cried.

"Soon," Joe assured her. "It has to end soon."

***

"April, what are you doing here?" Ed asked in surprise when he opened his door.

"From now on I'll be conducting my visits with Andrew here at his home. He is required to comply with unannounced visits, as well as scheduled ones. I see that he's behind you in the house now. May I come in?"

Ed squared up his shoulders. "No, you can't come in. I've had enough of all this legal crap. Leave us alone," he spewed as he attempted to close the door in her face.

April was quick, and stuck her foot in the door jamb to stop it from closing. "Mr. Preston, I am advising you to watch the way you speak to me while in the presence of your son. I am an officer of the court and you will respect me."

"An officer of the court?" Ed repeated as he opened the door wide and stepped out to meet her face-to-face. "You act like you're such a hard ass. You've got no hold over me. I want you off my property right now."

April stepped back, not sure what Ed's next move was going to be. She reached into her purse and pulled out a card. "Here's an appointment card for Andrew's mental health evaluation," she said, holding it out for Ed to take. "I took the liberty of selecting a provider and scheduling it for him. Have you selected a new sexual offender therapist yet? I know you wouldn't want your son to be in jeopardy of violating the court orders."

Ed stared at the card, jutted out his chin as he pivoted around, and slammed the door closed in her face. April shook her head at his ignorance and placed the appointment card in the mailbox before leaving. She went back to the office and immediately dialed Kate. "Hi, Mrs. Rose, it's April. How's Megan doing?"

"She's trying to cope. Therapy is good for her, but the progress she made previously has regressed since the second incident."

"I'm sorry to hear that. Listen, I just wanted you to know that an appointment has been made for Andrew to get his psychological testing completed. Ed doesn't know it yet, but there is a plan in place for the preventive care caseworker to show up at his house ready to bring Andrew there if Ed refuses to take him."

"You really think Ed is going to allow them to take his son for testing?"

"I have my doubts, but we need to show the judge that we tried everything to make sure Andrew complied with the requests. If Ed refuses, then we'll have to take action. I've mailed him a second copy of the parent responsibility section in Andrew's probation agreement. It clearly outlines that he needs to follow through with any and all recommendations made by the agencies on Andrew's case. We want Ed to know that what he agreed to in there is legally binding, and we will take necessary action if the conditions aren't met."

"I hope he complies, for his son's sake," Kate said.

"I'll call him the day before to remind him. In the meantime, you concentrate on getting your daughter's spirits up. Let me worry about Andrew."

"Thanks, April." Kate hung up the phone and went to the living room to join Megan, who was beating her stepdad at a cut-throat game of *Candy Land*. "I think we need a treat," Kate announced. "Who wants to go for ice cream?"

"I do," they both shouted in unison.

CHAPTER TWENTY-TWO

October 2001

Dear Mr. Edward Preston:

Today all the agencies currently involved in your son's care had a team meeting regarding Andrew and your refusal to cooperate with our services.

You have been previously notified that your son needs sexual offender counseling, and you have refused to allow him to have an updated assessment. If you do not have an updated sexual offender assessment scheduled within two weeks and provide your probation officer written verification of the evaluation, a probation violation hearing will be held. As of right now, the hearing is on the current court schedule, but I can have it removed if you comply with my requests. Your son also needs psychological testing, and you failed to comply with his scheduled appointments. This is also a violation of your son's probation.

As you are aware, Mr. Preston, the other day you called me a "dumb ass" and you referred to me as being a "hard-ass probation officer" in front of your child. Your continued demeaning manner to this officer in front of my client makes the supervision of your child on probation difficult. Please refer to the enclosed copy of the parental expectation version of your son's probation terms. You were also provided with a copy of this upon my initial meeting with you and your son.

This is your official notice that if you have not complied within two weeks to the terms of the probation agreement, a violation hearing will take place. This will put your son at risk of being removed from your care and placed into a foster home. Since you refused to take Andrew to the appointments due to the fact that we scheduled them for him, I am leaving it up to you to take the initiative and schedule new ones. I strongly urge you to follow through with these mandated assessments.

Thank you for your quick response,
Probation Officer April Monet
cc'd: Judge Lagoe
cc'd: Mrs. Kate Rose

Kate set her copy of the letter she received in the mail on the table and wondered why Ed would choose to play Russian roulette with his son's future. It seemed to her that his own selfish pride was more important than his child's welfare. She folded the letter, placed it back inside the envelope, and picked up the phone to call April.

"I'm sorry, Kate," she told her. "I know it wasn't Andrew's fault he missed the appointments. He's only twelve and has no way of getting there by himself, but I was left with no other option but to file probation violation charges against him for non-compliance."

Kate sighed deeply. "It's all a game to Ed. He's trying to prove his power and in doing so, he's putting his own son at risk."

"If I could charge Ed instead, I would in a heartbeat.

Never in my thirty years on the force have I seen anyone as deceitful and arrogant as he is. But since Andrew is the one on probation, the charges had to be filed against him. It will be the only way the court can get the services for Andrew."

"What if Ed still refuses to cooperate?"

"Simple. We'll place Andrew in foster care. My hope is a threat to take his son will prompt him to do the right thing."

"That's pretty drastic," Kate admitted.

"It is, but we've tried to get Andrew all the help he needs. Even the preventive-care caseworker has offered to take Andrew to the appointments so Ed wouldn't have to be bothered, but Ed refused to allow it. There is no excuse for Ed's actions. He only wants to control the situation. Now he's gotten himself in a position where his son could be taken away due to his ignorant behavior."

"Let me know what happens."

"You will be required to attend the court date as well," warned April. "Even though you do not wish to see Andrew, he is still your child and the judge will require you to be there."

Kate's stomach instantly clenched up. She hadn't set eyes upon Andrew since that fateful evening in August when he molested his sister in the pool, and violated the second chance she had given him. If she never saw him again, it would be too soon.

"I don't know if I can face Andrew. What will happen if I don't attend the hearing?"

"The judge will issue a warrant for your arrest. The papers are already in the mail and you have been summoned to attend. Like it or not, Kate, you will have to set your emotions aside and come to the hearing to testify."

Set my emotions aside? I am not only being forced to face my daughter's rapist, but I am also being forced to help put my son into a foster home. How am I supposed to pretend this doesn't mean anything to me?

"Okay, I'll be there," Kate relented. "I need to go April. I'll talk to you later."

Kate heard her say goodbye as she was hanging up, then ran to the bathroom and vomited.

***

Walking down the barren hallway leading to the courtroom was like walking through a nightmare and not being able to wake up. Kate's body went through the motions, but her mind tried to find a way to escape the desolate situation.

A representative from the Department of Social Services, April, Joe, Karen, and Kate all sat on one side of the courtroom while Ed and his mother, Maureen Preston, sat next to Andrew and the family court attorney on the other. The possibility of Andrew being placed in a foster home was very apparent, and the tension between the two sides of the courtroom could have been cut with a knife.

"All rise," the bailiff began. "The honorable Judge Lagoe, residing."

"You may be seated," the judge instructed. "The prosecution has provided me with sufficient document and proven beyond a reasonable doubt that Andrew is indeed in violation of his parole agreement, though vastly due to his father's actions. The court has no other choice but to remove him from his father's home and place him into foster care for a period of eighteen months. There is a spot available at the Fresh Start group home on the west side. During this time, the state will see to it that Andrew receives a mental health evaluation. While he is at the group home, and until discharged from the new provider, he will be attending Northside Treatment Center for his sexual offender counseling. This facility allows for a higher level of care, while still allowing Andrew to receive services on an outpatient basis. They will send me weekly updates on his progress."

"Your honor, what about visitations for my client?" Ed's lawyer asked.

"Mr. Preston, you will be allowed visitation with Andrew for two hours, twice a week. Mrs. Rose, you may visit per your discretion. Andrew will be placed in foster care directly following today's proceedings."

"No!" cried Ed as he grabbed Andrew. "You can't take him from his father."

"Mr. Preston, this could all have been avoided if you had followed the rules," reminded the judge.

"This is all your fault!" Maureen screamed at Kate. "He's going away because you refused to sweep all this under the carpet. I hope you're happy." She was close enough to her ex-daughter-in-law now that Kate could smell the outdated perfume on her aging neck. Kate inched closer to Joe and stared straight ahead.

Doesn't she realize all I did was bring her granddaughter down to the emergency room to make sure she was all right? I didn't call Child Protective Services. I wasn't the one who made all of those hotline calls. If her son hadn't refused to cooperate with the court, Andrew would still be in his care.

Ed moved in behind his mother, his eyes seared through Kate like they used to prior to one of his rages.

"Order in the court," demanded the judge. "Return to your seats at once."

They returned and huddled together near the defense table, their accusing eyes never veering off of Kate. When order was restored in the room, the judge continued. "It will cost two hundred dollars a day for Andrew's care while he is in the foster home. The state will need to recoup some of this money. Therefore, I am ordering each parent to pay seventeen percent of their income to help cover the cost."

Kate's lawyer, Mrs. Jackson, immediately rose. "Your honor, Andrew is only being placed due to his father's negligence in following the court's recommendations. Why should my client have to pay for his mistakes?"

"She is his biological mother. That makes her responsible regardless," he stated. "And since the seventeen percent from each parent is not enough to recoup the state's cost, I am also ordering Mr. Joseph Rose, Andrew's stepfather, to pay seventeen percent of his income as well."

Joe pounded his fist against the table. "I refuse to pay support for someone who abused my stepdaughter," he yelled.

"Mr. Rose," Judge Lagoe interrupted, "You will do as the court orders. You are married to the child's mother, which makes you responsible for Andrew as well."

Mrs. Jackson rose again. "Your honor, please be reasonable. You are asking the victim's family to pay twice. Not only would the money be coming from the same household, but it will be taking away from the victim. This is totally unfair."

"Whether you think it is unfair or not is irrelevant. Andrew has three adults who are responsible for him, and all of them are going to help cover the cost of his care. End of story. Now, we need to finalize the visitation order between Megan and her father," continued the judge.

"Your honor," interrupted Ed's lawyer, "My client has something to say before you make your decision."

"Proceed," he said.

Ed rose, crossing his hands in front of him as he spoke. "Your honor, I have been advised by my lawyer that it would be in my best interest if I agreed to give up all visitations with my daughter."

"You are volunteering to have your rights revoked?" clarified the judge.

"Yes. I can't take the chance of being alone with her and having another abuse report filed against me. I won't run the risk of jail time."

"If you are surrendering your rights on your own accord, then I will allow it. Mrs. Rose, you are hereby awarded full physical and legal custody of your daughter, Megan."

A steady stream of happy tears poured down Kate's cheeks. Joe grasped his wife's hand and bounced it up and down in a cheer of happiness. Victory for Megan was finally upon them. Their war was finally over. Joe hugged Kate tightly and whispered, "We did it, honey. She's safe."

"Mrs. Rose," Judge Lagoe interrupted the excitement, "even though Mr. Preston will no longer have visitation rights to his daughter, I do encourage you to reinstate a relationship between her and her father."

Kate furrowed her brows in confusion. "But he just gave up his rights to her. Doesn't that mean he can't see her anymore?"

"He voluntarily surrendered his rights, they weren't abolished," the judge corrected. "He can reapply for them anytime he wishes. In the meantime, the child still needs a father in her life."

Kate gestured toward her husband. "She has a father. My husband is the best father she has ever had. Never once has he hurt her."

"Mrs. Rose!" reprimanded the judge.

"I'm sorry, your honor. Yes, I will," she said lying through her teeth. *I most certainly will not! Never will I allow her to see him again. I just have to pretend I will until court is dismissed, then his rights will be officially terminated. Once we walk out of here, she will safe again. "Family above all" is not always the best option.*

"I'm glad we understand each other. Court is dismissed," concluded the judge as he left the bench and entered his quarters.

"You fucking bitch! You finally managed to get your son put away. I'll get you for this. You are going to pay!" screamed Ed so loudly Judge Lagoe rushed back in. Everyone in the room froze in their tracks to see what was going to happen.

"Bailiff, remove him at once," ordered the judge.

"Sleep with one eye open bitch, because I'm coming for you," screamed Ed as he was escorted out into the hallway.

Karen ushered her friend to a corner while Joe went into the hall to make sure Ed had left the premises. It didn't matter because Kate knew he was going to come after her as soon as they walked out those doors, and there would be no witnesses.

Kate's knees trembled so hard she could barely stand. "He's going to kill me. He will wait outside by his car and when I go out there, it will all be over with." Her voice broke as she spoke.

"He's not going to kill you because Joe and I are here to protect you," Karen assured her. "There are video monitors out in the parking lot. If there is a commotion, the security guard will be able to see it."

"I can't go out there," Kate mumbled through tears.

"Listen. Joe will go get the car and drive up to the door to get us. You won't have to set foot into the parking lot.

Kate nodded. She wanted to get out of there and as far away from the people who hurt her daughter as she could. Andrew brushed past her with a look of hatred in his eyes as he was being escorted to his new home. She watched him go, and felt a twinge deep within her chest.

"Let's stop at the store on the way home," Kate suggested to Joe and Karen. "There's something I need to do."

Joe waited until he was sure Ed had left the premises before pulling the car up to take Karen and Kate to the shopping center. Clothes, toiletries, and magazines filled the cart. Eighteen months' worth of amenities to last Andrew throughout his stay at the group home. He may not have appreciated his mother's efforts, but at least her conscience was clear knowing she was caring for him, and trying to make the transition easier; a final gesture for the child who came from her womb. They piled up the car and drove across town to what would be Andrew's new residence until he officially became a teenager.

Without even asking to see Andrew, Kate dropped off the packages with the house mother and turned around without looking back.

CHAPTER TWENTY-THREE

January 2002

"Mrs. Rose, I'm glad you could meet with us. Even if you aren't comfortable meeting with Andrew during his sessions, it's important to his recovery for you be involved at any level," his new therapist said during their first meeting.

"You must understand my hesitation in being here, and insisting it only happen when Megan was at school," Kate noted.

"I do, but the important thing is you're here now. Andrew's taken a big step in recovery. As part of a rigorous therapy regimen here at Northside, all clients are mandated to help create a safety plan for themselves. The center's mission is to make each person take ownership of their actions, and prevent them from re-offending in the future. It took Andrew two months to write a plan we would accept, and one he agreed to follow."

"So he fooled around for two months trying to get out of it," Kate clarified.

"He tried, but we didn't let him," the therapist responded. Take a look at his safety plan," he insisted.

<u>Andrew Preston's Safety Plan</u>

1. I will take part in structured activities such as group therapy sessions and socializing with other people.
2. I will be supervised at all times.
3. I will not babysit or be left alone with children who are younger or smaller than me.
4. I will stay away from pornographic material and magazines.
5. I will follow my supervision guidelines.
6. I will respect boundaries by keeping an arm's length distance at all times from other people, knock on closed doors, keep bathroom door closed when using it myself, always be fully clothed when sleeping and when not in bathroom, and I will be in a private location when I want to masturbate.
7. I will not be alone with my victim.
8. I will not form friendships or date anyone who is two or more years younger than me.
9. I will not play M rated video games or watch R

rated videos.

10. I will not utilize chat lines or sexual telephone services.

11. I will not use sexual words.

My high-risk warning signs that I may re-offend are:

1. Having other people introduced into my life such as parent's partners or their children.

2. Not knowing how to be around people I don't know too well.

3. Not getting along with mom.

4. Feeling hate toward parent's partners and their children.

5. Feeling hate toward mom

6. Feeling like people are trying to control me.

The high-risk situations I will avoid are:

1. Being around other people that I hate.

2. Being invisible to other people.

Kate's heart skipped two beats as she pushed the paperwork aside and stared at the wall. *Was Andrew saying he did these things because of his hatred toward me? If he were willing to sexually assault somebody out of rage, what else would he be willing to do as he got older and stronger? Would Megan or I be safe when Andrew was old enough to drive? Would he come back with a heart full of rage—thinking I had abandoned him and chose to keep Megan instead?*

"Mrs. Rose?" the therapist asked, trying to get her to focus back on the matter at hand.

"Yes," Kate answered.

"Your son worked really hard on writing this. It wasn't easy for him."

Kate rubbed the back of her neck to help relieve the growing tension. Seeing on paper what made Andrew tick was more than she could handle. "This isn't easy for me either."

"Do you want to exercise your rights to visit with him in foster care? It would be great if the two of you could reestablish a relationship."

"No," she answered quietly. "I gave him a second chance. He didn't take it. My heart has no more room for somebody who lacks so much empathy for others."

"Imagine how he must feel."

"What does he feel?" Kate blurted out. "Does he feel sorry? Guilty? Does he even care how much hurt he has put on this family?"

"Mrs. Rose, I wish I could answer that for you. We haven't had much luck getting him to open up yet."

"That's part of the problem. He doesn't talk about his feelings. Do you know how he's doing in the foster home?"

"I've gotten a few reports that he makes the female staff uncomfortable there. Even though Andrew created his safety plan, he does struggle with the terms of his agreement. He's unable to identify why he abused in the first place, and what he could do to ensure it will not happen again. This is something we work on during our time with him."

"So nothing's changed. He's in a new place, but still using sex as a weapon?"

"Mrs. Rose, at least with him in the state's care we will be able to get the psychological exam for the court and our center is working on the updated sexual offender evaluation. It's a step in the right direction."

"What about his father? Has he been cooperating with you?"

"Not really," he admitted. "We did try family counseling with the two of them, but Ed seemed to make Andrew nervous. He refused to answer anything without first looking at his father to see what his reaction was. We also noticed Andrew displaying nervous ticks when Ed was around. Eventually, we told Ed he wasn't welcome to participate anymore."

"And what about when the time is up? What is going to happen when his placement expires?" Kate asked.

The therapist set his clipboard down and placed his hand over Kate's. "He'll most likely be returned to his father," he admitted.

Kate shifted uncomfortably in her seat. "And do you think letting him go back to Ed is a good idea?" she asked. "You just said Ed is hindering Andrew's progress. Can't you write a note to the judge saying what you observed during sessions?"

"Of course we will, but it's always a good idea to keep families together."

Kate closed her eyes and cupped her head within her hands. "I don't understand," she moaned. "How do you plan on keeping everyone safe?"

"This safety plan is only the first step in the process.

Andrew will be required to write a detailed summary of the actual abuse, along with an apology letter to his victim. Once this is done, we will invite you in so he can read it to you."

"He has to recite to an audience how he abused his sister?" The heat in the room appeared to have risen exponentially. "I don't...know..."

"Mrs. Rose! Mrs. Rose!" Kate vaguely heard him scream as the room went dark. When she next woke, the therapist and two ladies were standing over her.

"What happened?" Kate whispered.

"You fainted, Mrs. Rose. How are you feeling?" one lady asked as she put her hand behind Kate's head and slowly helped her to her feet.

"I'm okay, thank you," Kate said sitting down at the table.

"The thought of having to listen to details of the abuse must have been too much for you right now," the therapist stated. "I will continue to have Andrew work on his admission. If you ever feel you are ready to hear it, we'll be able to facilitate it."

Kate nodded, knowing she would never be able to handle sitting in front of Andrew and listen to him talk about how he abused his little sister. "I need to go now," Kate murmured, picking up her purse.

"Are you able to drive?" the other lady asked.

"I'll be fine. I need to go." Kate hurried out of the office as fast as she could. Her heart pounded with each step. She scrambled through her pocket for her keys, unlocked the car, and drove until the sun faded from the sky.

She wanted to forget. Forget what she already knew of the abuse. Forget her life was in shambles. Forget she had a son who was a rapist.

CHAPTER TWENTY-FOUR

December 2002

As the Christmas holiday came upon them, Kate's motherly instincts kicked in. She felt guilty as she finished her holiday shopping and didn't get Andrew anything. Kate agonized as to whether or not she was expected to buy for him, even though she hadn't seen him since the day he left court and was taken to foster care. There was no way he deserved any presents; gifts would reward him for what he had done.

Kate wondered if she would be expected to buy a gift for an extended family member who had performed such vile acts against her daughter. Probably not, but she was Andrew's mother. Wasn't it her parental responsibility to provide for her child? This debate weighed on her so much it interfered with the peacefulness the holidays were supposed to bring. Kate finally made an appointment with Ann so she could help her sort out her feelings.

Ann listened to Kate as she explained the pros and cons of her dilemma. When Kate was finally quiet, Ann point-blankly asked her a question. "Do you want to buy him presents?"

Immediately, Kate responded, "No!" *Why would I want to spend time and effort picking out gifts for someone who hurt my family so much? I didn't even want to see this person anymore, let alone wish him happiness.*

"Then why are you even considering it?" she asked.

"I feel guilty, like it's something I'm expected to do. A mother is supposed to make her children happy at Christmas."

"I understand your reasoning, but if you don't feel it, then you shouldn't act upon it. Your time and affection that you choose to share with others is an earned privilege, not an expected one. You should never feel pressured into giving something your heart doesn't agree with."

Relief washed over Kate as she heard the words. She needed to let her burden go. Andrew felt no remorse for the atrocious actions he had done, and now she could finally come to terms with her own sense of guilt. No longer would she worry about the criticism from others for standing her moral ground. This turning point transformed her way of thinking and allowed her to refocus her life.

Ann handed Kate a tissue as she watched the release of emotions trickle down her cheek.

"Thanks," she sniffed back while drying her eyes. "I really needed to hear those words."

"Anytime you need to talk, my door is always open."

"I appreciate it."

"Now go give Megan a hug for me," she instructed.

Kate picked up her jacket and purse, then stood to offer Ann a hug. "Merry Christmas, Ann."

"Merry Christmas, Kate."

***

With a clear conscience, Kate was free to enjoy the rest of the holiday season. She made cookies for Santa with Megan and Joe, and when they decorated the

Christmas tree, Kate did not allow herself to feel guilty for leaving out the nine-years-worth of handmade ornaments Andrew had made for her at school. It was a big step for her toward moving on. She wanted this time to be joyful, as they deserved peace after all they had endured.

After the cookies had been frosted and put away, Kate went about the household chores. She went to her mailbox, retrieved the mail, and shook the snowflakes out of her hair once back inside. Kate slid off her mittens and boots, and placed the envelopes on the table while she warmed up some hot cocoa, then sat down with her mug and leafed through the mail. Christmas cards, utility bill, phone bill, and a letter from the Department of Social Services. Kate ripped open the envelope.

Office of Children and Family Services
Child Protective Intake Report
Case # 634092
Abuse/Maltreated Child: Andrew Preston
Alleged Suspect: Ed Preston
Intake Narrative:

Andrew is a thirteen-year-old child who is being denied basic food, clothing, and shelter while in the care of his father. The child Andrew also has not been receiving the mandatory Sexual Offender Therapy that was court ordered since his release from the state's care ten weeks ago. Suspicion of past neglect and possible abuse are noted.

Released from the group home? When did Ed gain custody back? The system had taken three months before they began to process her child support payments after Andrew was in the state's care. Since she was still paying, she assumed he was still there. *Why wasn't I notified of his release?*

Kate read the paper further and noticed Ed's address was listed just south of his previous home. *Ed found a loophole to make all of the past problems go away. I bet as soon as he got his son back he moved out of the county thinking the current court order for continued therapy wouldn't carry over to the new jurisdiction. He thought he could move away from his problems.*

Emotionally, Kate couldn't handle getting involved and tucked the paperwork away. The sound of the phone ringing pushed her thoughts aside.

"Hi, Kate, it's Maureen. Listen, I've really missed being able to see Megan for the past few months. I'm going to come pick her up and take her shopping for Christmas presents."

"Excuse me?" Kate asked, shocked that Ed's mom had the nerve to call after her outburst in the courtroom the last time they saw one another.

"Well, I am her grandmother and I have a right to see her. I'll be over in an hour," she said trying to not give Kate time to think.

"Tonight isn't good, Maureen. She's got dance class," Kate lied.

"Then I'll be over tomorrow night to pick her up."

Kate's stomach was turning knots. The idea of her daughter being alone with anyone on Ed's side of the family did not sit well with her. She let the phone sit in silence trying to come up with an excuse fast.

"Kate, are you still there?"

"I'm here," she whispered, wishing she wasn't.

"I haven't seen her in ages and I want to spend time with her during Christmas. Why are you making this so hard?"

Kate battled with her conscience for a few minutes more trying to figure out an easy solution that would satisfy both of them.

"If you want to see Megan, you are more than welcome to come over to the house to visit her, but I do not feel comfortable letting her go anywhere without me."

"Don't be ridiculous. I'm her grandmother. If you won't let me take her then I'll be forced to sue you for Grandparent's Rights and get a visitation schedule."

Kate froze in her tracks. *She wouldn't really file a petition against me, would she?* She told herself it was Megan's father and brother who had hurt Megan, not her grandmother, so Kate finally relented.

"Tomorrow night you can pick her up after dinner as long as it is going to be just the two of you," Kate clarified. "You can take Megan for two hours and then I want her right back home. That will give you more than enough time to shop."

"Two hours? You're being ridiculous. Two hours isn't enough time to do anything."

"It's two hours or nothing," Kate repeated. "And you are not to have Megan call her father on the phone or drive her anywhere to meet up with him."

"You're being overdramatic," she bellowed.

"Maureen, when did Andrew get released from the group home?" Kate asked, trying to change the subject.

"Almost three months ago. He was released early. Why?"

"Because I didn't know he was out."

"Well, he is and he's doing fine."

Kate picked the paperwork back up and read it over again. "Then why am I looking at a copy of a new Child Protective Services report that claims Andrew is being neglected?"

"I don't know anything about a report. Andrew has been the happiest he's ever been since being back with his father. Ed is doing a great job taking care of him."

"Then why would someone place a hotline call saying Andrew is being denied food, clothing, and shelter?"

"That's absurd," Maureen shouted.

"Well, I didn't make the call. Obviously someone involved in Andrew's life thinks he's being neglected. He's only been back in Ed's custody for a couple of months and he can't even care for him properly. What is he thinking?"

"I'm not having this conversation with you, Kate. Ed and Andrew are fine. They have a new place to live and a new life. Stop interfering with it. I'll be over tomorrow to pick up Megan. Goodbye."

Kate hung up the phone, suspicious that Maureen really knew more then what she was letting on.

The next morning when Kate told Megan her grandma wanted to take her Christmas shopping, she was more than excited to go. She spent the day thinking of all the new toys she would pick out for herself. Kate spent the day dreading when Maureen would pull in the driveway to take her daughter out of her sight. She knew Joe wouldn't approve of Megan going with her, so just this once she kept their plans a secret from her husband. It was Christmastime, and she wanted to keep the peace with everyone. At six o'clock that evening, they heard the knock on the door. Kate opened it to find Megan's younger cousin on the other side.

"Is Megan ready to go?" she asked.

Kate was livid. Not only had Maureen not come inside herself to get Megan, but she brought other people with her even after they agreed it would just be the two of them. *She claimed she was desperate to spend time with Megan because it had been so long since she'd seen her, so why would she bring someone else who was going to take away from the one-on-one time she wanted so badly?* Kate's gut was telling her to change her mind and not let her daughter leave her sight. Megan saw her cousin at the door and ran to give her a hug, which made Kate unable to bring herself to tell her she couldn't go. She kissed her goodbye and tousled her hair as she prepared to leave. "Have fun, honey. I'll be waiting for you when you get back."

"Bye, Mommy. I love you."

Kate forced a smiled and closed the door. *What have I done? I just handed my daughter over to the mother of the person who had abused her, and if anything happens to Megan, it will be my fault for allowing her to go.* Her head pounded as she envisioned all the possible scenarios that could arise. The two and a half hours they were gone were the longest of Kate's life. She considered going to the store to check up on them, but convinced herself she was being paranoid. Instead, she paced around the house until she saw the car lights pull into the driveway, a full half hour past the agreed upon time. Before Kate got to the door, she heard Maureen's car peel out—and then watched the tail lights disappear down the road as Megan walked through the door by herself, her hands full of new toys.

Why didn't her grandma walk her in?

"I saw my real dad and his new girlfriend," Megan professed as she set down the bag of toys she had just received.

"Really, where?" Kate asked, trying to maintain her composure.

"At the store. Grandma took me to meet him, and guess what, Mommy? He's nice now! He told me he never really hurt me and it's all your fault that he can't see me anymore."

Kate thought she felt a vein pop in her forehead. "Honey, why don't you take your new toys up to your room and play while I make a phone call."

"Okay," she said and ran upstairs dragging the bags behind her.

Kate dialed Maureen's cell phone number, but wasn't surprised when she didn't pick up. *She knows she was wrong. That's why she got out of the driveway as fast as she could, and why she's refusing to answer her phone. She's a coward and doesn't want to confront me.*

"Hi, this is Maureen. Leave a message at the beep."

"What the hell is the matter with you?" Kate screamed into the phone. "You brought your granddaughter to visit with a person whom the court has issued a no contact order against? The same person who sexually abused her? You put your own granddaughter at risk! Well, I hope it was worth it because you have just ruined your chances of ever seeing Megan again." Kate slammed the receiver back onto the handset so hard it ricochet off and fell to the floor.

As mothers, Maureen and Kate never saw eye to eye. Maureen needed to protect her son to the very bone, no matter what he did. Kate felt you had to teach your children between right and wrong. Maureen refused to believe any of the accusations brought against Ed and Andrew, even though Andrew confessed to the crimes, and Kate had shown her the report from Child Protective Services that stated they knew both Ed and Andrew had touched Megan. Maureen still denied it. Her boys were innocent in her mind and she would always be there to protect them. Perhaps if she had made her child accountable for his actions in the past, he wouldn't be in the situation he was today.

***

"I can't believe you let her take Megan," Joe exclaimed when he came home from work. "Do you know how lucky you are that Maureen brought her back at all? Anything could have happened. If they had chosen to keep her, it would have been your fault for handing her over."

"I know. I didn't know what else do to. I can't spend my whole life worrying about what may or may not happen. Let's count our blessings that she was unharmed." As an optimist, Kate always tried to see the good in people, but this quality clouded her judgment as a mother. She vowed to never again be so gullible when it came to her daughter.

Kate was mad at Maureen for tricking her into letting her take Megan to see her father, but most of all Kate was mad at herself for allowing it to happen. Kate was serious about never letting Maureen into Megan's life again. When she called the following week asking to take Megan to a Christmas party, Kate refused to allow it. Three weeks later, a lawsuit for visitation based on Grandparent's Rights was filed with the court against Kate. Her lunch reconnected with her throat as she read the petition.

I wish to be granted visitation rights every other weekend, and two weeks during the summer so I can take my granddaughter to see her father and brother. The child's mother was instructed by the court to encourage a relationship with her father and has failed to follow through on this recommendation because of her own feelings toward my son. She will not even allow me to take photographs of my granddaughter for me to share with my family. I will take it upon myself to see that father and daughter are reunited once again.

Kate could not believe this woman was wasting the court's time to bring together a sexual abuse victim and her offenders. It shouldn't have surprised her though, seeing how she had wanted Kate to sweep the whole thing under the carpet to begin with.

"Joe," Kate yelled from the dining room. "Come here. We have a problem," she warned, reading the paper over again.

Joe turned off the television and came into the dining room. Her hands shook as she showed him the new petition. His face grew red, but he didn't say a word as he marched out of the room. A few minutes later, he returned with a business card in one hand and the phone in the other. He dialed the number of his old acquaintance, and put it on speaker so Kate could hear what his lawyer had to say.

"It's very hard to prove Grandparent's Rights," Rick stated. "When there is a visitation schedule set up between the parents, any visitation between grandparent and child is usually done during the time when the opposite parent has the child. So, Ed's mother would get to see Megan when Ed has her for visitations. But since Ed's visitations have been suspended by the court and you have sole legal and physical custody, Maureen would have to prove you were somehow unfit. She doesn't stand a chance in the courtroom, but since the papers have been filed the courts are obligated to hear her plea."

Joe flashed his wife a smile. "Thanks, Rick. We'll stop down tomorrow and drop off the petition so you can review it before we step into the courtroom."

"No problem. I'll contact Megan's law guardian and schedule an appointment for them to meet. Don't worry; we'll do all we can to keep Megan safe."

Joe hung up and kissed his wife's forehead to reassure

her. Kate's mind knew Maureen didn't stand much of a chance, but her nerves were on end knowing what happened the last time they were in the courtroom together. She didn't want to be anywhere near Maureen, or her son. Ed's family had issues Kate didn't want any part of, yet they maintained a hold over her she could not seem to escape.

One week before the court date, Megan's law guardian, Chelsea, stopped by the house to talk with her about the upcoming litigation. With Megan slightly older now, she was able to voice her opinion and have the judge take her own wishes into consideration. The petition papers were read and explained to her and then she was asked what she thought about them.

"I don't want to see my Grandma," Megan announced.

"Why not?"

"She wants to take me to see my dad and brother. They're mean, I don't want to see them."

"Is that what you would like me to tell the judge when we go to court next week?"

"Yes. I want to stay with my mom, not go with Grandma."

"Well, I'm glad we got to talk about this, Megan, because you should be able to help decide what it is you want."

"Okay," she answered, rising up from her chair. "Can I go play now?"

"Sure, honey. I need to talk with your mom and stepdad for a little bit."

Megan ran into the living room and turned on the television. Kate waited until she knew Megan was fully immersed before she asked Chelsea how heavily Megan's wishes would influence the judge.

"I think the chances are pretty good the judge will consider them. She was pretty clear on her intentions of not wanting to go with either grandma or dad. I'll be at the hearing and I'm going to recommend the petition gets thrown out."

"Thank you," Joe sincerely stated. "This has been going on way too long and our little girl is finally at a place in her life where she is starting to feel safe and we need to keep it that way."

"I agree. No child should be forced to go with a person he or she is not comfortable with. To be safe, I'm going to have Ann write something as well so the judge will have both our recommendations against it," Chelsea concluded.

"Thank you. We'll see you in court," Kate added as she walked her to her car.

The next week was so stressful the nights and days blended together with only a thin layer of sleep between them. Kate worried about her daughter being forced to go back to a place where she felt unsafe, and she struggled to clear her mind of all the possible things that could happen to Megan while she was there. It was the longest wait of Kate's life.

Walking hand in hand to what would hopefully be their last visit to the courthouse, Joe voiced his confidence that they would soon be able to put the past behind them. Kate, however, remained skeptical this was how they were going to spend the rest of their lives. Once they made their way through the metal detectors and headed toward the registration desk, Joe nudged Kate as they walked past the two waiting rooms.

"Why is Ed in one room and his mother in the other?" he asked.

"Are you kidding me? Why would they do that?" Kate snapped.

"They're playing mind games with us."

"Well, I refuse to sit in either waiting room. We'll stand here in the hallway until they call our name."

From the corner of her eye, Kate could see Ed had noticed they were standing in the hall. She wasn't about to let him think he was bothering her, so she quickly flashed Joe a smile as they stood as casually as possible. Kate couldn't figure how it would have benefited them to sit separately; no logical explanation came to mind. When their case was called, Joe and Kate lingered and watched as Ed and his mother emerged from their separate rooms and entered into the courtroom without a single word to each other.

"All rise," the bailiff ordered as the judge found his way into the courtroom and sat at the bench. "You may be seated." Ed walked to the bench in the back of the room, leaving his mother to sit alone at the table.

"We are here to answer the petition about granting visitations to the paternal grandmother of Megan. Can you tell the court why you felt it necessary to bring us here today, Mrs. Preston?"

"I have not seen my granddaughter for several months. Her mother has alienated us from her life. All I want to do is bring my family together again." Maureen looked as if she was about to cry.

"It would be your son's responsibility to ensure his daughter had time to visit with you, not her mother," informed the judge before he turned his focus to Ed.

"Sir, as of right now you have no legal rights to visit with Megan. Would you like to petition the court to reestablish visitations so you may take her to go see your mother?"

Ed remained at the back bench, but stood to answer the judge. "Your honor, I am tired of all this. My mother brought me here against my will and is trying to force me into taking my daughter again. I can't do this anymore. My son and I are trying to start a new life. I do not wish to have it turned upside down again. No, I will not ask the court to allow me to see my daughter again."

Kate's heart fluttered with happiness. Ed had announced his surrender, giving them an end to a treacherous battle that had held her daughter's safety at stake for way too long. Gleaming, Kate squeezed her husband's hand and listened as the judge concluded the arguments.

"Without your son's willingness to regain rights to his daughter, then your requests for visitations are moot. This case is dismissed."

Maureen shot Ed a disgusted look and mouthed four letter words at him. He glared at his mother and extended his middle finger toward her.

Joe leaned in and kissed Kate on the lips. "You're free," he cheered, clasping her hand within his.

"I love you, Joseph Rose. Thank you for seeing me through this."

Smiling at his wife, he placed a gentle hand on her face. "I wouldn't have had it any other way."

They headed out the door and never looked back. Megan was safe and Kate's mind was finally at ease knowing Ed wanted to move on. She looked up at the sky and smiled at the rainbow arcing over the clouds; a symbol of peace and good things to come.

EPILOGUE

May 2012

Holding the brown paper bag tightly over her mouth, Kate panted heavily in a state of hyperventilation. She wasn't sure if this is where she wanted to be, or if her presence would make a difference.

"This doesn't get any easier, does it?" Karen asked.

Kate shook her head and lowered the bag enough to show her best friend the glaze in her eyes was clearing up. "Thanks for coming, Karen. You've seen me through thick and thin. I couldn't do this without you."

"Look around, Kate. Do you see the sign over the door? The End Violence Against Women International Conference! You are sitting here in San Diego, California, with hundreds of people waiting to hear you talk. The strength from people like you has inspired every one of them to stand up and reclaim their lives."

Kate glanced around, in awe of the number of people who had turned out for the event. "Pretty amazing, huh? Who would have thought just a few years ago I felt ashamed and was hiding under a rock?"

Karen hugged her friend tight and handed Kate the

microphone. "Go get 'em, sweetie." Taking one last deep breath, Kate Rose walked to the podium with confidence.

"Good morning, everyone. Thank you for coming. I spent days trying to prepare my speech for you. I wanted to find just the right words to convey my message. Once my trash bin was filled with the crumpled papers of my attempts, I realized I only needed to speak from the heart." She paused and stole a glance at her husband, who gave her a thumbs up from the side of the stage, then refocused on the audience in front of her.

"Several years ago, I found myself at a crossroads where few before me stood. I knew no matter which path I took, my life would be forever altered, and no choice would be the easy choice. I had to ask myself, should I disregard what happened simply to keep my family intact, or do I stand up for my moral integrity and choose to go down the road less traveled because it's the right thing to do? I knew not everybody would understand my decision, nor did I expect them to.

The night my daughter was sexually abused was a defining moment in my life. It was my job as a parent to protect her at all cost. She needed to know somebody was going to save her from further abuse, fight for her rights, and shield her from the pain. I took this job seriously.

As a parent, I was left with both anger and grief that my daughter had her innocence stolen from her. While my emotions were overwhelming to me, they were generally understood by others. Society often views the parents of a victim with sympathy and compassion.

But there is another side to stories of sexual abuse, the side rarely spoken of—the side of those forgotten mothers out there, whose sons committed the crimes. They are left with unanswered questions and guilt over the choices their children made. Behind these forgotten faces are the mothers who are forced to live with remorse, and wish their children could get the help they desperately need.

I am both of those mothers. My adversity began when my twelve-year-old son sexually abused his younger, autistic sister. I am the mother of girl who was sexually abused, and the mother of her rapist. I was forced to choose between my two children, and this is my story."

The crowd drew silent, as if taking in every word. The next hour Kate shared her family secrets with them, not holding back any details. It felt good to talk about things, as though saying the words were releasing her from her mental prison.

Finally, Kate turned over the last page of her notes and opened the floor to discussion from the eager audience. The first question came from a petite young lady who had been taking notes during the entire speech.

"Do you still live your life in daily fear?"

Kate smiled. That was an easy answer. "No. Life has started to become calm for the first time in many years. Our times spent in the shadows of the justice system are behind us, and not a single word has been heard from either Ed or Andrew since our last day in court over ten years ago. It all seems very abnormal to me, but we are enjoying it immensely. The chaos I had become accustomed to in the past has disappeared, and my family is now experiencing the so-called normal life I have only heard others talk about."

A reporter from CNN who was covering the conference stood to ask his question. "Does your daughter still have difficulties dealing with the abuse she endured?"

"The effects of the abuse still linger, but no longer rule her life. Recovery is a slow process, one that perhaps is never complete. Megan and I are both in better places now. This doesn't mean we forgot what we have lived through; it means we have learned to live despite what we endured. Our past does not define our future; it only serves as a stepping-stone that allows us to move to places we have never been. We are stronger now with a determination to bring a positive outcome out of a deep family tragedy.

She is so amazing, that daughter of mine. Beautiful, resilient, and loving. I wasn't sure if she would ever be able to recover, yet each morning she wakes up with a smile on her face. She is a survivor in every sense of the word. Her past does not hinder her ability to see the good in the world and I am amazed every day at her strength."

Kate noticed a young woman in the audience whose eyes appeared to scream out for help as she spoke. Kate offered her the floor. "How long did it take your family to recover?" she asked in a soft voice.

"Years have now come and gone, and Megan's strength continues to grow. She is looking forward to the day when I will buy her a beautiful white gown so she can walk down the aisle to marry the man of her dreams. She wants to have children and be a good mom to her babies. The fact that she has been able to move beyond her fear of boys and dresses, and wants to nurture her own children in the future tells me she is no longer a victim. My daughter is a true survivor. She is thriving because somebody stood up for her, and showed her she was worth more."

"How do you cope knowing you have another child out there that you don't have any contact with?" A shorthaired woman asked.

"Never in a million years would I have thought one day I would walk away from my firstborn child. But here I stand, raising only one of the children I birthed—my daughter. Life is unpredictable, but I am proud that I fought for my daughter. Given the circumstances, it was one of the hardest things I ever had to do. No mother wants to choose between her own children, but I cannot carry the guilt of Andrew's actions. He was the one who chose to abuse other children, and it was his choice to abuse his sister again after I gave him a second chance. These were his actions, and I have come to accept that I had no control over them. I can only take responsibility for what I did to try to prevent it from happening again." Kate paused and glanced at the clock in the back of the room. "I have time for one last question," she noted.

Instantly, a flurry of hands flew up. Kate gave the floor to another reporter. "Do you think your son is remorseful for his actions?"

"Does Andrew regret hurting his sister? I'll probably never know. I pray he has learned from his mistakes and will never put another person through that kind of pain again. Maybe if he finds remorse within himself, it will allow him to grow as a human being. I will always wonder what drove him to abuse in the first place. Was it a reaction to the divorce as one therapist claimed, or had he become a victim himself? Maybe someday I will learn the answers and be able to piece together why our lives were turned into shambles. Until then, I have come to terms that we are a family no more. We are divided by morals and values, a distinct line that I refuse to cross. There are plenty of other families out there teetering on the very same line. I hope they, too, find the strength to cross over, and help save a child from being abused any more. This is the reason why I am here today—to give strength to parents facing such adversity, and to give hope for the victims still living with their secrets.

We, as a society, need to erase the stigmatism that is attached to sexual abuse and start talking about the real issue. Once we break the silence, we will take the power away from the abuser and put it into the hands of the victims, and in turn start preventing anyone from having to experience the anguish ever again. If just one person walks away with the courage to speak up about his or her own situation, then telling my story here today will have been worthwhile. Thank you for allowing me to stand before you today and to be part of your healing journey."

Kate carefully placed the microphone back onto the podium, and walked toward Joe and Karen. They met her halfway with a large bouquet of red roses wrapped with a teal ribbon, the symbol for sexual abuse survivors. Kate wiped her eyes, and smiled at the two people who had supported her unconditionally through the worst years of her life.

"Let's go give these to Megan," Kate said with a smile.

www.ingramcontent.com/pod-product-compliance
Lightning Source LLC
Chambersburg PA
CBHW051753040426
42446CB00007B/338